The Bible and the Qur'an

The Bible and the Qur'an

Biblical Figures in the Islamic Tradition

John Kaltner and Younus Y. Mirza

t&t clark

LONDON • NEW YORK • OXFORD • NEW DELHI • SYDNEY

T&T CLARK
Bloomsbury Publishing Plc
50 Bedford Square, London, WC1B 3DP, UK
1385 Broadway, New York, NY 10018, USA

BLOOMSBURY, T&T CLARK and the T&T Clark logo are
trademarks of Bloomsbury Publishing Plc

First published in Great Britain 2018
Reprinted 2018

Cover design: Freer Gallery of Art and Arthur M. Sackler Gallery,
Smithsonian Institution, Washington, DC: Purchase—Charles Lang
Freer Endowment, F1946.12.188

A catalogue record for this book is available from the British Library.

ISBN: HB: 978-0-5676-6601-7
PB: 978-0-5676-6600-0
ePDF: 978-0-5676-6602-4
ePub: 978-0-5676-6603-1

A catalogue record for this book is available from the Library of Congress

Typeset by Newgen KnowledgeWorks Pvt. Ltd., Chennai, India
Printed and bound in Great Britain

To find out more about our authors and books visit
www.bloomsbury.com and sign up for our newsletters.

Contents

Acknowledgments

During the 2016 spring semester, I taught a course titled Biblical Figures in the Qur'an that gave me the opportunity to reflect on pedagogical issues related to the content and design of this book. I thank the students in that course for their efforts, enthusiasm, and many helpful comments and ideas as we worked through the material together. Among those taking that course was Katie White, who was my student research assistant at the time, and I appreciate very much the many discussions she and I had about the course and this book. Debra Bartelli continues to support and inspire me in everything she does, and I dedicate this book to her with love.

John Kaltner

I want to thank my parents, M. Yaqub Mirza and Tanveer Mirza, for supporting my educational and academic endeavors. My dad always encouraged me to focus on my education and helped support my studies in the Middle East and during graduate education. My mom has been a constant inspiration and source of spiritual support; she consistently reminds me to keep in mind the bigger picture and to look at the long-term prospects. My wife Rehenuma Asmi has been a wonderful companion. I could not have finished this book without her encouragement and friendship.

Younus Y. Mirza

Introduction

Non-Muslims are often surprised to learn that many people who are mentioned in the Bible play important roles within Islam. In fact, some of the figures from the past who are revered most by Muslims are also held in high regard by Jews and Christians because of their prominence in biblical literature. Muslims agree with their fellow monotheists about the importance of these individuals because of their understanding of revelation. Islam teaches that throughout history, prophets have been sent to deliver a message from God to their people, and many of those messengers—like Abraham, Moses, and Jesus—are referred to in the Bible. Consequently, the lives of these prophets are held up as models to be valued and respected because they have provided guidance and insight about God's will for humanity.

This book offers an overview of how biblical figures are presented in two key Islamic sources that are familiar to all Muslims. The first is the Qur'an, the sacred text of Islam, and the other is a set of writings known as "The Stories of the Prophets." These sources not only examine the lives of well-known prophets like those cited above, but they also sometimes refer to less prominent individuals who are found in the Bible. When we refer to the Bible, we are speaking about the books that comprise the Hebrew Bible, the Old Testament and the New Testament. The nearly fifty entries in this book discuss people who are mentioned in both biblical literature and Islamic sources. Most entries look at a single person, but in a few cases—like angels, Jews, and Christians—larger groups are considered. Each entry examines key passages from the Qur'an that treat the individual or group, and many of them include some discussion of how they are presented in "The Stories of the Prophets." In some cases, "The Stories of the Prophets" literature has nothing or very little to say about a person or group, and so those entries describe only how they are presented in the Qur'an. Each entry concludes with some questions for discussion and suggestions for further reading. Throughout the book, people's names are written both in English and in a transliteration of their Arabic forms. The English translations of Qur'an passages are our own, and the citations from "The Stories of the Prophets" come from the works mentioned below. The remainder of this introduction provides some background information on the Qur'an and "The Stories of the Prophets."

The Qur'an

The sacred text of Islam is closely tied to the life of the Prophet Muhammad (570–632 CE), who was from the western part of the Arabian Peninsula in what is now Saudi Arabia. According to the traditional account of his life, around the year 610 CE Muhammad had the first of a series of revelations from God that continued intermittently throughout the rest of his life. Islam teaches that the Qur'an is an accurate record of the messages that Muhammad received from God through the angel Gabriel during that twenty-two-year period. The word "Qur'an" (also spelled "Koran") comes from the first word directed to Muhammad—*iqra'*, an Arabic command that means "Recite!" The term "Qur'an" means "recitation," which underscores the book's nature as an oral text that is meant to be proclaimed and heard aloud. The Qur'an is the oldest literary text in the Arabic language.

A central theme throughout the Qur'an is the need to follow and obey the will of the one God. This idea is so important that it was used to designate the religion that emerged from the Qur'an and those who follow it—the Arabic word "islam" means "submission," and a "muslim" is one who submits. The call to monotheism was not well received by many in Muhammad's earliest audience because they were predominantly polytheists, and so he and his early followers were sometimes persecuted by those who did not accept his message. They eventually left the city of Mecca, Muhammad's birthplace, for a town some two hundred miles to the north that had invited Muhammad to serve as a judge who would help resolve disputes among its inhabitants. That town, which later became known as Medina, was more open to Muhammad's message, and it was there that the Muslim community began to develop and flourish. The migration from Mecca to Medina in 622 CE, known as the *Hijrah* in Arabic, was such an important event that it marked the beginning of the Islamic calendar.

The Qur'an is comprised of 114 chapters of varying lengths that contain a total of approximately 6,300 verses, which is about the same number of verses found in the New Testament. In this book those chapters are identified by numbers, but each one also has a title that is a word, name, or theme found in the chapter. For example, chapters 2, 4, 5, 14, 19, 29, 65, and 101 also go by the names "The Cow," "Women," "The Table," "Abraham," "Mary," "The Spider," "Divorce," and "The Disaster," respectively.

The chapters of the Qur'an are not arranged chronologically but by length, with the longest ones coming first. The Qur'an begins with a brief introductory chapter called "The Opening," and this is followed by the longest chapter in the book, which has 286 verses. Chapter 108 is the shortest chapter, with only three verses. The lack of a chronological arrangement can be seen in the fact that the command *iqra'* mentioned earlier, which tradition says is the first word revealed to Muhammad, begins chapter 96. An important distinction is made between the chapters that were revealed in Mecca during the early part of Muhammad's prophetic career, and those from the later time when he was in Medina. In general, those from the Medinan period tend to be longer, while the Meccan ones are shorter. This means that if one wants to get a general sense of how the Qur'an developed over time, it would be best to start with the shorter chapters and read the text backward. The decreasing length of the chapters throughout the Qur'an can be seen in a recent English translation of the text in which the first 57 chapters comprise 375 pages, while chapters 58 through 114 take up only 85 pages.

Muslims believe that the original Arabic form of the Qur'an is the only true version of it and that a translation is not actually the Qur'an but simply an interpretation. One reason for this is that the Arabic text is written in rhyming prose in which the last word of each verse in virtually every chapter ends in the same or a similar sound. Such a consistent rhyming pattern is impossible to duplicate in another language, and Muslims consider it to be an essential aspect of the text. Even those who do not know the Arabic language are struck by the beauty of the Qur'an when they hear it proclaimed by someone trained in the art of Qur'anic recitation. Since less than 20 percent of Muslims worldwide speak Arabic as their first language, most are not able to understand the Qur'an in its original form. In those places where Arabic is not spoken, when the Qur'an is read aloud, in mosques and other public settings, it is first proclaimed in Arabic and then translated into the local language. This explains why there are so many bilingual versions of the text that contain Arabic in one column and a translation in the other.

Given Islam's monotheism and emphasis on God's unity, the Qur'an's use of plural first-person pronouns like "we," "us," and "our" in divine speech can strike the non-Muslim reader as unusual and unexpected. An example of this can be seen in the first verse of chapter 97, where God explains how the Qur'an was revealed—"We sent it down on the Night of Glory." Interpreters throughout history have consistently agreed that this language does not violate the oneness of God that is central to Muslim belief. Most see it as a stylistic device that exalts God in a way similar to the royal "we" or divine "we" found in other cultures and texts. For example, in the first chapter of the biblical book of Genesis God says, "Let us make humankind in our image, according to our likeness" (1:26).

The Qur'an often appears to be a confusing book to those who have not read it before, and this can be especially true for Bible readers, who expect it to follow the structure and style of their own sacred text. Because it does not unfold in chronological order and it sometimes shifts topics and modes, the Qur'an can seem haphazard and random to the newcomer. But in recent times, scholars have challenged this view by identifying structures and patterns within individual chapters or sections of them that indicate they are carefully organized units that took shape in response to the social and religious contexts of the early Muslim community. It is therefore important that non-Muslims avoid using the Bible or other texts as a yardstick by which to evaluate the Qur'an.

This is particularly the case when considering the Qur'an's presentation of the biblical figures who are the focus of this book. The parts of the Qur'an in which they are mentioned will have an air of familiarity for Bible readers as the events in the lives of biblical characters are recounted. But how they are discussed in the Qur'an can also raise questions because the Islamic text never presents the stories in the same way as in their biblical counterparts. Sometimes the differences are small and subtle, but elsewhere they can be quite significant. In general, the Qur'an presents the biblical figures in a way that conforms to Islamic beliefs and practices, and this is a feature of the text that will be seen repeatedly throughout this book. Those familiar with the Bible must be attentive to the reasons behind this presentation of the characters and stories, which is not due to animosity or disrespect toward Judaism and Christianity. The Qur'an relates the stories about these figures in ways that allow them to serve as models for Muslims about how to accept the message of Islam and submit oneself to the will of God. Therefore, rather than viewing the Bible and the Qur'an as competing with one another, the stories about Abraham, Moses, Jesus, and others within them should be seen as shared traditions that speak to different communities in diverse ways in order to address each one's unique concerns and contexts.

Although material related to biblical figures plays a key role in the Qur'an, it is important to keep in mind that this book contains only selected portions of the text and it does not give a true sense of the content and style of the entire Qur'an. The themes and subject matter of the passages discussed here are representative of the book as a whole, but they are only a starting point. In order to get an accurate sense of the full text one should read the Qur'an in its entirety, and at the end of this introduction several English translations of it are listed as additional works to consult.

"The Stories of the Prophets"

"The Stories of the Prophets" literature frequently fills in perceived gaps or embellishes certain parts of the Qur'anic narratives in order to give the stories more narrative flow and to entertain their readers. In the summaries of these sources, the focus is on two things: (1) the key themes that the different authors speak to; and (2) the observations that they make regarding the relationship between the Qur'an and the biblical tradition. The summaries are not meant to be exhaustive, but they aim to give a picture of how the genre has understood the figures cited and to draw attention to key issues or debates that emerge from the stories. Including the authors' perspectives is essential because it shows how Muslims have imagined and reimagined the prophets throughout history and in light of their own circumstances. In the entries, the names of the authors of "The Stories of the Prophets" are identified in parentheses.

The second part of many entries summarizes how the individuals and groups are presented in some of the important Muslim Stories of the Prophets literature, in particular the works of al-Kisā'ī (d. 6th/12th century), al-Tha'labī (d. 427/1035), al-Ṭarafī (d. 454/1062), Ibn Kathīr (d. 774/1373), and al-Nadawī (1914–1999). The details of much of al-Kisa'ī's life remain unknown, but the hallmark of his Stories of Prophets is its narrative flow in which he often weaves biblical material into the Qur'anic presentation. Al-Tha'labī was a product of Nishapur in modern Iran, and he was known for his exegetical scholarship on the Qur'an. Al-Tha'labī's Stories of the Prophets distinguishes itself by its literary quality and its entertaining nature, which also incorporates biblical material into the various narratives. Al-Ṭarafī was an Andalusian scholar who specialized in the variant readings of the Qur'an. His Stories of the Prophets work represents his diverse milieu, and it is characterized by its mystical interpretations. Ibn Kathīr lived in medieval Damascus and was a scholar of Qur'anic exegesis, Islamic law, history, and prophetic reports (ḥadīth). His Stories of the Prophets is highly dependent on those reports, and it is unique in that it often compares the Arabic Bible with the text of the Qur'an. Abū ḤaHsan al-Nadawī was a modern Indian scholar who specialized in a number of Islamic disciplines ranging from ḥadīth to histories. His Stories of the Prophets work is distinctive in that it is written in an accessible style and was part of his larger project of modern Muslim revival.

Additional Resources

English Translations of the Qur'an

Droge, A. J. trans., *The Qur'an: A New Annotated Translation* (Sheffield/Bristol: Equinox, 2013).

Haleem, M. A. S. Abdel. trans., *The Qur'an: A New Translation* (Oxford: Oxford University Press, 2005).

Nasr, Seyyed Hossein, et al. trans., *The Study Qur'an: A New Translation and Commentary* (San Francisco: HarperOne, 2015).

Further Reading on the Qur'an

Ernst, Carl. W. *How to Read the Qur'an: A New Guide, with Select Translations* (Chapel Hill: University of North Carolina Press, 2011).

Esack, Farid. *The Qur'an: A User's Guide* (Oxford: Oneworld, 2005).

Haleem, Muhammad Abdel, *Exploring the Qur'an: Context and Impact* (London: I. B. Tauris, 2017).

Mattson, Ingrid. *The Story of the Qur'an: Its History and Place in Muslim Life* (Oxford: Blackwell, 2008).

McAuliffe, Jane Dammen. ed., *The Encyclopaedia of the Qur'an* (6 vols.; Leiden: Brill, 2001–2006).

Reynolds, Gabriel Said. *The Qur'an and Its Biblical Subtext* (New York: Routledge, 2010).

Further Reading on "The Stories of the Prophets"

Klar, M. O. *Interpreting al-Tha'labī's Tales of the Prophets: Temptation, Responsibility and Loss* (New York: Routledge, 2009).

Mirza, Younus Y. "'Was Ibn Kathīr the Spokesperson for Ibn Taymiyya?' Jonah as a Prophet of Obedience," *Journal of Qur'anic Studies* 16 (2014), 1–19.

Mirza, Younus Y. "Ibn Kathīr, 'Imād al-Dīn," *Encyclopedia of Islam 3rd edition*, ed. Kate Fleet, Gudrun Krämer, Denis Matringe, John Nawas and Everett Rowson (Leiden: Brill, 2017).

Qureshi, Jawad Anwar. "Nadawī, Abū al-Ḥasan," *The Oxford Encyclopedia of Islam and Politics*, ed. John Esposito and Emad el-Din Shahin (Oxford: Oxford University Press, 2017).

Saleh, Walid A. *The Formation of the Classical Tafsīr Tradition: The Qur'ān Commentary of al-Tha'labī (d. 427/1035)* (Leiden: Brill, 2004).

Tottoli, Roberto. *Biblical Prophets in the Qur'an and Muslim Literature* (New York: Routledge, 2002).

Tottoli, Roberto. "New Sources and Recent Editions of *Qiṣaṣ al-anbiyā'* Works and Literature," in *Legendaria medievalia: En honor de Concepción Castillo Castillo*, ed. R. G. Khoury, J. P. Monferrer-Sala and M. J. Viguera Molins (Cordoba: Ediciones El Almendro, 2011), pp. 525–39.
Wheeler, Brannon M. *Prophets in the Qur'an: An Introduction to the Qur'an and Muslim Exegesis* (London/New York: Bloomsbury Academic, 2002).

Websites

http://al-quran.info/#home
This website contains the text of the Qur'an in Arabic, in addition to a transliteration of the Arabic, translations of it into many languages, and audio of numerous recitations of the text.

http://corpus.quran.com/
The Qur'anic Arabic Corpus website at the University of Leeds explains the Arabic grammar, syntax, and morphology for each word in the text, and it also contains multiple translations of the Qur'an into English.

http://expositions.bnf.fr/parole/index.htm
The *Torah-Bible-Coran* website of the Bibliothèque Nationale de France in Paris, available in both French and English, contains images of and information about the Bible and the Qur'an. Click on each image for details about it.

1

Aaron/Hārūn

Qur'an 37:114–20; 21:48–49; 23:45; 28:34; 20:29–34; 26:13; 20:70; 7:120–22; 26:46–48; 7:142–57; 20:83–98; 19:28

Aaron's name is Hārūn in the Qur'an, where he is mentioned twenty times in thirteen different chapters, and is described as assisting his brother and fellow prophet Moses/Mūsā. Aaron/Hārūn is rarely named in the text without an accompanying reference to Moses/Mūsā, and a summary of their prophetic careers is presented in 37:114–20. According to that passage, God favored them and rescued them and their people. The deity guided them both by giving them the "clear book," likely a reference to the Torah. Among the other gifts God bestowed on the brothers are light, a message for believers, signs, and authority (21:48–49; 23:45).

The Qur'an recounts the burning bush episode in several places, and in most of them Moses/Mūsā asks God to appoint Aaron/Hārūn to be his helper and accompany him when he goes to Pharaoh/Firʿawn to seek his people's freedom. In one of those texts, Moses/Mūsā claims that Aaron/Hārūn possesses oratorical skills that he himself lacks. "My brother Aaron is a more eloquent speaker than I am. Send him with me as an assistant who will confirm me, for I fear they will accuse me of lying" (28:34; cf. 20:29–34; 26:13). When they come before Pharaoh/Firʿawn to persuade him to let the Israelites go, Aaron/Hārūn plays a less active role than his biblical counterpart does in the plagues narrative in Exodus 7–11. Nonetheless, the Egyptian magicians acknowledge his involvement when, after being astonished at the signs the brothers perform, they prostrate themselves and express their belief in "the Lord of Aaron and Moses" (20:70; cf. 7:120–22; 26:46–48).

As Moses/Mūsā prepares to ascend the mountain on which he will commune with God for forty days, he asks Aaron/Hārūn to take his place and lead the people while he is away (7:142). The golden calf episode, which is described twice in the Qur'an, shows how Aaron/Hārūn had difficulty filling his brother's shoes and fulfilling his request (7:148–57; 20:83–98). The account in chapter 7 (which does not identify Aaron/Hārūn by name) is closer to the biblical story in Exodus 32, but Aaron's/Hārūn's character comes across as less culpable in the Qur'an then he is in the Bible. When Moses/Mūsā returns from the mountain and angrily confronts him, Aaron/Hārūn claims that he was overpowered by the people and could do nothing to stop them. This causes Moses/Mūsā to offer a prayer to God for forgiveness for himself and his brother (7:150–51). His inability to control the people indicates that Aaron's/Hārūn's sin in the Qur'an was one of omission, rather than one of commission. His role is reduced in the other version of the story, but it quotes the words Aaron/Hārūn directs at the people in his effort to convince them not to worship the calf (20:90). The connection between Aaron/Hārūn and the priesthood, which is a key part of his characterization in the Bible, is not mentioned in the Qur'an.

One verse in the Qur'an posits a sibling relationship, perhaps a symbolic one, between Aaron/Hārūn and someone other than Moses/Mūsā. In 19:28 Mary/Maryam, the mother of Jesus/ʿĪsā, is addressed as "sister of Aaron/Hārūn." It is unclear whether or not this is a reference to the brother of Moses/Mūsā. If so, the word "sister" should not be understood literally because Mary/Maryam lived at a much later time period. It could be a way of speaking about her as a family member who was a descendant of Aaron/Hārūn, or perhaps as his sister in faith by virtue of their belief in the same God. It is also possible that the name Aaron/Hārūn refers to a biological brother, who shares a name with the prophet of the past and is otherwise not mentioned in the Qur'an.

Questions/Issues

(1) What are some possible reasons why the Qur'an does not connect Aaron/Hārūn with the priesthood?
(2) Identify the most significant differences in the ways Aaron/Hārūn is depicted in the golden calf story as it is told in Exodus 32 and in Qur'an 7:148–57.
(3) What is the most plausible explanation for why Mary/Maryam is referred to as "sister of Aaron/Hārūn" in the Qur'an?

Further Reading

Reynolds, Gabriel Said. *The Qur'an and Its Biblical Subtext* (New York: Routledge, 2010), pp. 132–34.

2

Abraham/Ibrāhīm

Qur'an 4:125; 3:67, 95; 6:161; 16:123; 2:135; 22:78; 16:120–21; 19:48–50; 21:70–71; 2:124–29, 260; 11:69–73; 15:51–60; 29:31; 51:24–37; 11:74–76; 37:99–113; 6:74–83; 19:41–50; 21:51–71; 26:69–86; 29:16–27; 37:83–98; 43:26–27; 60:4

Abraham/Ibrāhīm is mentioned nearly seventy times throughout the text of the Qur'an, and only Moses's/Mūsā's name appears more frequently in the book. The biblical story of Abraham/Ibrāhīm is rather lengthy (Gen. 11–25) and some of the episodes it contains are found in the Qur'an, but the Islamic text lacks the narrative detail present in the biblical accounts of those events. The Qur'an also recounts some traditions about Abraham/Ibrāhīm that do not have biblical parallels, although in some cases they are related to material found in nonbiblical Jewish sources. A title the Qur'an uses for Abraham/Ibrāhīm that is also shared by both the Hebrew Bible and the New Testament is "friend of God" (4:125; cf. Isa. 41:8; Jas 2:23).

The Qur'an presents Abraham/Ibrāhīm as a true believer who, even though he predated the Prophet Muhammad by centuries, is the prototype for all Muslims to follow because he lived his life in complete submission to God's will. His exemplary character is summed up in this verse, which explains both what Abraham/Ibrāhīm was and what he was not. "Abraham was not a Jew or a Christian, but he was an upright person who submitted and was not one of those who associate" (3:67). Because he lived long before both Judaism and Christianity, he should not be identified with either of those religions. He was also not someone who committed the sin of *shirk*, or association, by violating the unity of God and associating something or someone in creation with the uncreated deity. Abraham/Ibrāhīm is described in this verse as a *ḥanīf*, which is translated as "upright person," and is often understood to be someone who practices monotheism. The word *ḥanīf* appears twelve times in the Qur'an with eight of them referring to Abraham/Ibrāhīm, who is the only person identified this way by name in the text. In eleven of its twelve occurrences, the term *ḥanīf* is immediately followed by a reference to someone who associates (*mushrik* in Arabic). In this verse and in others like it, Abraham/Ibrāhīm is being held up as the quintessential believer who is the antithesis of the worst kind of sinner (3:95; 6:161; 16:123).

The important role that Abraham/Ibrāhīm plays as a model believer can be seen in another way in 3:67. The Arabic word that is translated here as "who submitted" is "muslim," a term that describes a person who engages in the act of submission that gives the religion of Islam its name. The verse reflects the belief that, long before the coming of Muhammad, prophets like Abraham/Ibrāhīm and their followers were living lives of submission to God's will. This is why Muhammad is repeatedly told in the Qur'an that he should follow the "religion of Abraham/Ibrāhīm"—his task was not to found a new faith, but to call people back to the way that God had intended for humanity from the beginning. "Then We revealed to you (Muhammad) to follow the religion of Abraham, who was an upright person and was not one of those who associate" (16:123; cf. 2:135; 3:95; 6:161; 22:78).

In the verses prior to the one just cited, there is another reference to Abraham/Ibrāhīm as a *ḥanīf* who was not a *mushrik* that contains a wordplay in Arabic that is impossible to duplicate in translation but which provides a good illustration of the literary artistry of the Qur'an. At the end of 16:120 it is stated that Abraham/Ibrāhīm was not someone who "associated," and the beginning of the next verse says that he was "thankful." The two words used in the passage sound alike in Arabic because they contain the same root letters in slightly different order—the verb "to associate" comes from the root *sharika*, while the verb "to thank" comes from *shakara*. Words built on these two roots follow one right after another in the Arabic text as verse 120 ends with a word from *sharika* and verse 121 begins with one from *shakara*. Through this use of the similarity in the sounds of the words, the Qur'an makes its point more memorable— Abraham/Ibrāhīm was not guilty of *shirk* (association) because he practiced *shukr* (thankfulness).

As noted above, the Qur'an refers to a number of events in the life of Abraham/Ibrāhīm that are also related in the Bible, and in some cases these episodes are described more than once in the Islamic text. Abraham/Ibrāhīm leaves behind his family and homeland to journey to a new land (19:48–50; 21:70–71; cf. Gen. 12:1–6), where he sets up a shrine for worship (2:124–29; cf. Gen. 12:8; 13:18). God instructs Abraham/Ibrāhīm to enact an unusual ritual that involves the division of animals and/or birds into parts (2:260; cf. Gen. 15:7–11). In both texts, Abraham/Ibrāhīm is visited by messengers sent from God who tell him that he and his wife will have a son, and then the messengers announce their plan to destroy the city where Lot/Lūṭ is living (11:69–73; 15:51–60; 29:31; 51:24–37; cf. Gen. 18:20–33). Prior to the city's destruction, Abraham/Ibrāhīm makes a plea to God in an effort to save Lot's/Lūṭ's people (11:74–76; cf. Gen. 18:22–33). Finally, in both the Bible and the Qur'an Abraham/Ibrāhīm nearly sacrifices his son, but in each case it turns out to be a test from God and the son is spared (37:99–113; cf. Gen. 22:1–19). An interesting aspect of how the last story is presented in the Qur'an is the fact that the son is not named in the text, and his anonymity has led to a discussion among commentators as to whether it was Isaac/Isḥāq or Ishmael/Ismā`īl.

Among the traditions about Abraham/Ibrāhīm in the Qur'an that do not have equivalents in the Bible, the most commonly cited one explains how he attempted to sway his people from polytheism and reinstitute monotheism among them. These stories sometimes describe his destruction of their idols, and Abraham's/Ibrāhīm's father is often present as his main antagonist (6:74–83; 19:41–50; 21:51–71; 26:69–86; 29:16–27; 37:83–98; 43:26–27; 60:4). This tradition from Abraham's/Ibrāhīm's life, which is also found in nonbiblical Jewish sources, is mentioned repeatedly in the text because it closely mirrors the Prophet Muhammad's experiences and it addresses issues that were of personal concern to him and the early Muslim community.

The version of the story in 19:41–50 describes the lengthiest conversation and encounter between Abraham/Ibrāhīm and his father, and is therefore the most poignant in terms of the picture of intergenerational conflict that it paints. It opens with Abraham/Ibrāhīm begging his father to reject polytheism and reminding him of the consequences if he fails to do so (vv.42–45). Four times throughout his plea he utters the words "My father!" which is how three of the four verses begin. After asking his father why he serves something that can neither see nor hear, Abraham/Ibrāhīm offers to share his own insight in the hope of guiding the older man. He then begs his father not to serve Satan/Shayṭān, and he expresses his fear that God will punish him if he continues to do so. The father's reply is shocking in its bluntness and for what it signals about the rupture in the parent/child relationship. Rather than respond in kind and address him as "My son," he calls Abraham/Ibrāhīm by name, physically threatens him, and tells him to get out of his sight. "Are you forsaking my gods, oh Abraham? If you do not stop this I will stone you. Leave my presence for a while!" Abraham/Ibrāhīm obeys his father's order to depart, but not before he wishes him peace and tells him that he will ask God to forgive him. "I will separate myself from you and from what you call upon that is not God, and I will call upon my Lord. Perhaps in calling upon my Lord I will not be in distress" (v.48).

Much in this story reflects Muhammad's situation, especially early in his prophetic career. He was orphaned at a very young age, and so Abraham's/Ibrāhīm's experience of separating himself from his father is not one that Muhammad could have known. Nonetheless, many passages in the Qur'an refer to the problems he encountered while trying to spread his message among the Meccans of his time and the often unfavorable reception he received as a result. Similarly, Abraham's/Ibrāhīm's forced withdrawal from his native land due to its inhabitants' unwillingness to accept his message mirrors Muhammad's own experience in 622 CE when he and a small group of followers had to leave Mecca out of fear for their lives and journey to the town of Yathrib that later came to be known as Medina. Just like the later prophet of Islam, Abraham/Ibrāhīm experienced rejection due to the inability of those close to him, represented here by his own parent, to put aside their idolatrous ways and follow the one true God. In this way, his story is told in conformance with the prophetic paradigm that is commonly found throughout the Qur'an, whereby the lives of prominent figures of the past are presented in ways that support and validate Muhammad's claim to be a prophet.

Abraham/Ibrāhīm is also presented as Muhammad's precursor in another tradition mentioned in the Qur'an lacking a biblical or Jewish parallel. According to 2:124–29, Abraham/Ibrāhīm and Ishmael/Ismāʿīl built and purified a structure meant to serve as a place of worship to God. This is commonly interpreted to be a reference to the Kaʿba, a shrine predating Islam that presently sits in the center of the Great Mosque in Mecca, toward which Muslims face five times each day when they pray. According to this passage, the Kaʿba traces its origin to the time of Abraham/Ibrāhīm and his son, who constructed it as a place for prayer to the one God. It eventually became a polytheistic site, only to be returned to its original purpose during Muhammad's lifetime when the people of Mecca embraced the monotheistic message of Islam that he preached. The references in the text to those who walk around the building and those who prostrate themselves (v.125) describe the ritual activities that Muslims engage in at the Kaʿba to the present day. The text closes with several prayers uttered by Abraham/Ibrāhīm and Ishmael/Ismāʿīl that also make connections with the later Muslim community that will worship on the site (vv.127–29). They first ask God to accept the building from them. They then request that both they and their descendants might be a community of people who submit to God, using terms that are etymologically related to the Arabic words for "Muslim" and "Islam." Finally, in a clear allusion to the coming of Muhammad and the Qur'an many centuries in the future, they pray that God will raise up a messenger from among their descendants, who will be given a book that will teach them wisdom.

In the Qur'an, Abraham/Ibrāhīm serves as the paradigmatic believer for Muhammad and the Islamic community. He is the prototypical Muslim, and every person must strive to be a *ḥanīf* like him and avoid being a *mushrik*. As the verse reminds them, all are exhorted to take Abraham/Ibrāhīm as their model and conform to his standard. "Truly, there is a good example for you in Abraham" (60:4).

In "The Stories of the Prophets," Abraham's/Ibrāhīm's birth story is recounted in which he is protected from harm by God and, as a newborn, stands up and proclaims, "There is no god but God, Who has no partner." He recites this same phrase on various occasions as he grows up and challenges the polytheism in the place of his birth. A significant portion of the account of Abraham's/Ibrāhīm's early life describes his conflict with Nimrud, the local ruler and a self-proclaimed deity, who refuses to accept Abraham's/Ibrāhīm's monotheistic message. He tries to confront and fight the God of Abraham/Ibrāhīm, but loses his life in the attempt. "The Stories of the Prophets" also explain how the local people attempt to kill Abraham/Ibrāhīm for his opposition to their religious practices, going so far as to catapult him into a raging fire that is too hot for anyone to approach. But God miraculously protects the prophet, who is able to walk away from the inferno completely unscathed.

Also recounted is a tradition in which Abraham/Ibrāhīm attempts to pass off his wife Sarah as his sister before a foreign king that is similar to the biblical stories in Genesis 12 and 20. Most of the focus, though, is on the relationship between Abraham/Ibrāhīm and Sarah's servant Hagar that is not mentioned in the Qur'an. It is reported that after a dispute between the two women, Abraham/Ibrāhīm brought Hagar and their son Ishmael/Ismā`īl to Mecca, where the shrine of the Ka`ba then lay in ruins. He left them there and returned after Hagar's death, when he came to visit Ishmael/Ismā`īl and his wife. Father and son then rebuilt the Ka`ba and engaged in several cultic activities that are part of the Muslim pilgrimage ritual to this day.

Another story in "The Stories of the Prophets" is related to the passage from the Qur'an mentioned above in which Abraham/Ibrāhīm dismembers birds. This tradition is cited to explain how Abraham/Ibrāhīm learned a lesson about the resurrection of the dead when the bird parts came together and reconstituted themselves. An additional story describes how Abraham/Ibrāhīm came to have faith in God while praying in a mountain cave. This mirrors closely the story about how the Prophet Muhammad came to embrace monotheism, and is a demonstration of how "The Stories of the Prophets" sometimes contain traditions that affirm and legitimate Muhammad's status as a prophet. (al-Kisā'ī; Ibn Kathīr)

Questions/Issues

(1) How closely does Abraham's/Ibrāhīm's character in the Qur'an match its counterpart in the Bible?
(2) Abraham/Ibrāhīm is presented in the Qur'an as the prototypical Muslim whose life should be emulated. Does his biblical character play a similar role in Judaism and/or Christianity?
(3) One of the most well-known scenes in the Bible about Abraham/Ibrāhīm is the near sacrifice of his son Isaac/Isḥāq in Genesis 22. What are the most important similarities and differences between the biblical account of that event and the one depicted in the Qur'an (37:99–113)?

Further Reading

Bakhos, Carol. *The Family of Abraham: Jewish, Christian, and Muslim Interpretations* (Cambridge: Harvard University Press, 2014).
Garsiel, Bat-Sheva. "The Qur'an's Depiction of Abraham in Light of the Hebrew Bible and Midrash," in *The Convergence of Judaism and Islam: Religious, Scientific, and Cultural Dimensions,* ed. Michael M. Laskier and Yaacov Lev (Gainesville, FL: University of Florida Press, 2011), pp. 45–63.
Levenson, Jon D. *Inheriting Abraham: The Legacy of the Patriarch in Judaism, Christianity, and Islam* (Princeton: Princeton University Press, 2012).
Lodahl, Michael. *Claiming Abraham: Reading the Bible and the Qur'an Side by Side* (Grand Rapids, MI: Brazos Press, 2010), pp.1–24.

3

Adam/Ādam

Qur'an 2:28–39; 7:10–25; 15:19–48; 20:115–22; 38:72–76; 6:1; 7:54; 41:9–10; 14:32–22

Adam/Ādam is the first human being created by God in the Qur'an. He is considered to be a prophet in Islam, but the Qur'an does not explicitly give him this designation. Adam/Ādam is cited by name eighteen times in the text, and in seven other places humanity is referred to by the phrase "children of Adam/Ādam." There are multiple accounts of the creation of humanity in the Qur'an, with slight variations among them (2:28–39; 7:10–25; 15:19–48; 20:115–22). Adam/Ādam was created from the dust of the earth, which is described as mud or clay (3:59; 7:12). God's hands (38:75) were used to form him, and then the deity breathed the spirit of life into him (15:29; 38:72). The reference to the divine hands, as well as other anthropomorphisms that are used to describe God in the Qur'an, have been discussed frequently by Muslim commentators, and it is generally held that they are not meant to be taken literally.

The Qur'an lacks a detailed account of Adam's/Ādam's creation, and there is no description of how the first female was made. God taught Adam/Ādam the names of all the animals, and then ordered the angels to bow down before the first human (2:30–34). They all did so except for one who is identified as Iblīs, who considered himself superior to Adam/Ādam because he was created from fire while the human being was created from clay. The Qur'an contains several versions of Iblīs' act of defiance, which led to his being banished from God's presence (7:11–12; 15:29–33; 17:61; 18:50; 20:116; 38:72–76). Iblīs' expulsion is followed by a description of the first couple's offense that led to their own removal from paradise.

Adam's/Ādam's unnamed mate is known as Eve/Ḥawwā' in other Islamic sources. The account of their time in the garden in 7:10–25 contains all of the key elements that are part of the tradition in the Qur'an: (1) God places them in a garden to live, where the deity forbids them to eat the fruit of a particular tree; (2) a deceitful agent convinces them to eat of the tree, whereupon they realize they are naked and become ashamed; (3) they have a final conversation with God in which they acknowledge their offense; and (4) they are then expelled from the garden. The forbidden tree is not identified in chapter 7, but in another passage it is described as the "Tree of Immortality" (20:120). The figure who is responsible for deceiving the couple is consistently presented as Satan/Shayṭān, and it is generally held that this is another way of referring to Iblīs. Upon discovering their nakedness, the couple attempt to cover themselves with leaves from the garden (7:22), but it is also stated that God provided them with clothing after their expulsion (7:26).

In the description of their offense, no distinction is made between the man and the woman as they act in tandem each step along the way (7:20–22). Their mutual involvement throughout the course of the story is underscored in the original text of the Qur'an by a distinct feature of Arabic grammar—verbs, nouns, and adjectives can be written in a dual form that refers to the actions or qualities of two people. In this case, twenty-eight words are grammatically dual in just four verses (7:19–22), highlighting the point that both Adam/Ādam and Eve/Ḥawwā' were fully involved in the events and equally culpable for the outcome. Upon being confronted by God for eating the fruit, they both acknowledge their mistake and beg for forgiveness (7:23). The deity then sends them to earth, which is described as a temporary place of enjoyment from which they will eventually be brought forth after their deaths (7:24–25). There is therefore an element of divine mercy in their expulsion from the garden, since it comes about in response to the couple's plea for compassion on God's part.

The version of the garden story in 20:115–22 is the shortest in the Qur'an, but it contains most of the same elements found in the account in chapter 7. Iblīs' role is reduced somewhat and Eve/Ḥawwā' is a secondary character as the focus is on Adam/Ādam, who appears to represent humanity as it is broadly conceived. The first and last verses of the passage suggest that the main theme of the story is divine forgiveness in the face of human beings' weakness and failure in their relationship with God. The deity reminds and advises Adam/Ādam to remain faithful, and then spells out the consequences if he fails to do so (20:117–19). Similarly, Satan/Shayṭān poses a question to him and does not deceive the couple outright (20:120), suggesting that the issue of human free will and choice is a central motif in this version of the story. In this account God is not asked to forgive the offense, but the deity nonetheless responds by choosing, returning to, and guiding Adam/Ādam (20:122).

While the texts do not mention Adam/Ādam by name, several other passages in the Qur'an share certain features with the biblical account of creation in Genesis 1. God is described in 6:1 as the one responsible for creating heaven and earth, and darkness and light. Elsewhere, the deity has the power to speak things into existence (16:40). The Qur'an does not provide a day-by-day account of how the world came about, but some texts point to a six-day process (7:54; 41:9–10). Human beings, as the "children of Adam/Ādam," hold a privileged place in the world that makes them special and sets them apart. The various elements of creation, including rivers, the sun, the moon, day, and night, are all described as being subjected to humanity (14:32–33). Despite this high status, however, the passage is quick to point out that this is all in accordance with God's will—it is ultimately only by God's authority that human beings have a privileged place over the rest of creation. That idea comes out clearly in a title God uses to describe Adam/Ādam in 2:30, where he is called a *khalīfah*. This Arabic term, often translated as "successor" or "vice-regent," is commonly used to refer to someone who rules in place of or on behalf of someone else, and it is a reminder to Adam/Ādam and his offspring that any authority they enjoy is temporary at best, and that they themselves remain subject to God and the divine will.

"The Stories of the Prophets" provide dramatic details regarding the creation of Adam/Ādam and his eventual fall. The storytellers speak about how the angels and jinn were initially skeptical of the creation of Adam/Ādam because a previous creation had created mischief and caused bloodshed in the universe. Some detail how God taught Adam/Ādam all of the human languages and the names of all things. Others connect the creation of Adam/Ādam with the advent of Muhammad. In one story, when Adam/Ādam opened his eyes, he saw written on the throne of God the Muslim testimony of faith, "There is no God but God, and Muhammad is his messenger" (al-Kisā'ī). In another tradition, Adam/Ādam wanted to be with Eve/Ḥawwā', but the angels prevented him from doing so until he paid her dowry. Adam/Ādam then asked, "What is her dowry?" The angels replied, "To pray for Muhammad, peace and blessing be upon him, three times." Adam/Ādam then asked, "Who is Muhammad?" They responded, "He is the last of the prophets from your sons. If it was not for Muhammad, you would not have been created" (al-Tha'labī). According to this tradition, Adam/Ādam was created only to prepare for the eventual coming of the Prophet Muhammad.

The commentators sometimes embellish the fall narrative in their descriptions of how Adam/Ādam was eventually expelled from paradise. Drawing from biblical narratives, many of the authors adopt the idea that Satan/Shayṭān appeared to Adam/Ādam in the form of a serpent that had four legs. The serpent first deceived Eve/Ḥawwā', who was then able to manipulate Adam/Ādam into eating from the forbidden tree. However, some scholars note the differences between the biblical and Qur'anic narrations, such as the fact that the serpent encourages Eve/Ḥawwā' to eat from the tree and that she is the one who feeds the fruit to Adam/Ādam. As discussed above, in the Qur'an only Satan/Shayṭān is mentioned, not the serpent, and both Adam/Ādam and Eve/Ḥawwā' initially eat from the tree. Moreover, in the Bible Adam/Ādam and Eve/Ḥawwā' are made aware of their nakedness, while in the Qur'an they were both clothed and then their clothes were taken away from them (Ibn Kathīr).

The Bible further appears in the theological discussion regarding whether the garden that Adam/Ādam and Eve/Ḥawwā' were in was the garden of paradise. For some scholars, paradise was supposed to be eternal, and it was a place that Satan/Shayṭān was prohibited from entering. However, in the creation story Adam/Ādam and Eve/Ḥawwā' are both expelled from the garden after Satan/Shayṭān approaches and converses with them. Many scholars thus held that the garden of Adam/Ādam and Eve/Ḥawwā' was not the eternal paradise, and they reference the Torah in support of this interpretation (Ibn Kathīr).

"The Stories of the Prophets" also emphasize Adam's/Ādam's regret for eating from the forbidden tree. In one tradition, Adam/Ādam cried and prostrated himself for forty years until God finally accepted his repentance (al-Ṭarafī). In another, Adam/Ādam made the same cry of repentance that the Prophet Jonah/Yūnus did, "There is no God but you. Glory be to you. Verily, I am one of the wrongdoers" (al-Kisā'ī). Like other prophets, Adam/Ādam is a model of repentance through acknowledging his mistake and returning to God. Thus, while "The Stories of the Prophets" literature differs on some of the details of the garden story, it agrees that God eventually forgave Adam/Ādam, that he was one of the righteous ones, and that he was the first prophet.

Questions/Issues

(1) Compare and contrast the accounts of human creation in 2:28–39; 7:10–25; 15:19–48; and 20:115–22. How are they similar to and different from each other? How are they related to what is described in Genesis 2–3?

(2) How would you summarize the Qur'an's view of human nature and humanity's place in the world?

(3) Is there anything about Islam's understanding of Adam/Ādam that is at odds with Jewish and Christian ideas about him?

Further Reading

Klar, M. O. "Through the Lens of the Adam Narrative: A Re-consideration of *Sūrat al-Baqara*," *Journal of Qur'anic Studies* 17/2 (2015): 24–46.

Pregill, Michael. "Isrā'īliyyāt, Myth, and Pseudepigraphy: Wahb b. Munabbih and the Early Islamic Versions of the Fall of Adam and Eve," *Jerusalem Studies in Arabic and Islam* 34 (2008): 215–84.

Roded, Ruth. "Human Creation in the Hebrew Bible and the Qur'an—Feminist Exegesis," *Religion Compass* 6/5 (2012): 277–86.

4

Angels

Qur'an 2:102; 35:1; 2:97–98; 66:4; 3:42–51; 2:30–34; 7:11; 15:29–30; 32:11; 13:23–24; 6:93; 8:50; 74:26–31; 43:74–78; 69:13–18; 40:7–8; 89:21–23

The Qur'an's cosmology includes nonhuman beings that are capable of interacting with people even though they are not part of the natural world that humans inhabit. The jinn are one such group, and angels are another. The singular form of the Arabic word for "angel" (*malak*) appears thirteen times in the Qur'an, while the dual form is found twice and the plural nearly seventy-five times. Among the angels mentioned by name in the text, Michael/Mīkāl and Gabriel/Jibrīl are biblical figures, while Hārūt and Mārūt are unique to the Qur'an. The latter two are mentioned in 2:102, where they are identified as two angels from Babylon who are associated with witchcraft and magic.

According to the Qur'an, the primary distinction among angels is the number of wings they possess, a difference that could be related to the different functions they serve. "Praise be to God, the creator of the heavens and the earth, Who made angels messengers with two, three, or four (sets of) wings. He adds to creation as He wishes, and God has power over everything" (35:1). This verse indicates that angels in Islam, as in the Bible, are primarily messengers. They often play this role in the text, but they are also present in other contexts in which they do not serve as heralds. The most prominent example of a messenger angel in the Qur'an is Gabriel/Jibrīl, who is mentioned three times in the text and communicates to Muhammad the message he receives from God (2:97–98; 66:4). Angels also play a prominent role as messengers in a scene in 3:42–51 that describes how Mary/Maryam is told she is pregnant and will give birth to Jesus/`Īsā. A group of angels appear to her to announce that she will bear a child, and then they tell her some of the things that Jesus/`Īsā will teach and do during his lifetime. In the scene just prior to this one the angels appear to Zechariah/Zakarīyā to inform him that despite their advanced ages, he and his wife will have a son—John/Yaḥyā, known as the Baptist in the New Testament.

Angels were present with God when humanity was first created, but they disagreed with the divine plan because of the problems that humans would create. Nonetheless, God showed a special preference for humanity by telling Adam/Ādam the names of the animals and other things in creation and withholding that information from the angels. When the deity then commanded the angels to bow down before Adam/Ādam, all but one (Iblīs) did so, indicating human superiority over the angels (2:30–34; cf. 7:11; 15:29–30).

Other contexts in which angels are mentioned in the Qur'an are in references to death and the end of the world. The angel of death is responsible for bringing each person to God for judgement, and whether the outcome is good or bad, angels will continue to interact with people in the afterlife. "Say, 'The angel of death who is in charge of you will summon you, and then you will be returned to your Lord'" (32:11). Angels will comfort and attend to those who are rewarded in paradise (13:23–24). At the same time, they will taunt unbelievers as they writhe on their deathbeds (6:93), and physically abuse those who are punished in hell (8:50). According to the Qur'an, nineteen angels stand guard over hell (74:26–31), where the main attendant, named Malik, refuses to listen to the pleas of the tormented (43:74–78). Eight angels will hold up God's throne at the end time (69:13–18; cf. 40:7–8), and row upon row of them will be present for the cataclysmic events that will occur then (89:21–23).

Questions/Issues

(1) Is the Qur'an's description of angels primarily a positive one or a negative one?
(2) When the roles of angels in the Qur'an and the Bible are compared, are the similarities between the two more obvious or the differences?
(3) How can the differences between how the Bible and the Qur'an present angels be explained?

Further Reading

Kassim, Hussain. "Nothing Can Be Known or Done without the Involvement of Angels: Angels and Angelology in Islam and Islamic Literature," in *Angels: The Concept of Celestial Beings —Origins, Development and Reception,* ed. Friedrich Vinzenz Reiterer, Tobias Nicklas and Karin Schöpflin (Berlin: Walter de Gruyter, 2007), pp. 645–60.

5

Cain/Qābīl and Abel/Hābīl

Qur'an 5:27–32

These are the two sons of the first human couple Adam/Ādam and Eve/Ḥawwā'. The brothers are unnamed in the Qur'an, where their story is told in 5:27–32, but they are identified as Qābīl and Hābīl in other Muslim sources. They are also not differentiated in the Qur'an on the basis of their occupations or the sacrifices they offer to God. The wording of the Arabic text allows for the possibility that only one sacrifice was offered by both of them. God accepts the offering as being only from Abel/Hābīl, and this causes Cain/Qābīl to murder his brother. He is aided in killing Abel/Hābīl by his *nafs*, a term that can mean "soul," "self," or "mind" (v.30).

After his offering is not accepted, Cain/Qābīl tells his brother that he will kill him (v.27). This leads Abel/Hābīl to speak his only words in the Qur'an, as he calls attention to his piety and expresses his desire that Cain/Qābīl be held accountable for his evil actions.

> God accepts from the pious. If you extend your hand against me to kill me, I will not extend my hand against you to kill you. I fear God, the Lord of the universe. I wish you would bear the sin committed against me and your other sins, and be one of the people of the fire. That is the reward for those who are wrongdoers. (vv.28b-29)

The account concludes with an etiological comment that explains the effect that Cain's/Qābīl's act of fratricide had on those who came after them. After the murder, Cain/Qābīl observes a raven sent by God scratching on the ground, and this makes him feel remorse and ask for repentance because he did not bury his brother's body. The deity does not speak at all in the story, and God's only act is to send the bird. According to the Jewish text *The Targum of Jeremiah*, a raven showed Cain the manner in which he should bury his dead brother. "Because of this, We laid it down for the children of Israel that whoever killed a person, except in the case of punishment for murder or causing corruption in the land, it would be as if he had killed all people. And whoever saved a person, it would be as if he had saved all people" (5:32a). The phrase "the children of Israel" is commonly used in the Qur'an in reference to the Israelites during the biblical period, but given the brothers' status as the offspring of the first human couple the lesson of the story is likely directed to a wider audience. With its closing statement, the story of Cain/Qābīl and Abel/Hābīl in the Qur'an becomes a tale of universal significance that has ramifications for future generations.

"The Stories of the Prophets" literature draws upon the biblical literature to discuss why Cain/Qābīl killed Abel/Hābīl and the larger lessons that the death has for humanity. One popular story relates that Adam/Ādam would not permit fraternal twins to marry each other but, rather, he allowed his children to marry one of their siblings from a different pair of twins. Abel/Hābīl was the older brother, and he wanted to marry the sister of Cain/Qābīl who was very beautiful. However, Cain/Qābīl wanted to marry his own sister. Adam/Ādam ordered Cain/Qābīl to give his sister to Abel/Hābīl so he could marry her, but Cain/Qābīl refused. Adam/Ādam then commanded them to provide an offering, and then he went off to make the hajj pilgrimage in Mecca. When they went to find their offerings, Abel/Hābīl came back with a fat portion of meat, while Cain/Qābīl brought back a poor portion of grain. Abel's/Hābīl's offering was accepted by God, while Cain's/Qābīl's was not accepted. Seeing this, Cain/Qābīl became furious and his jealously finally boiled over as he threatened his brother, "Verily I will kill you so you do not marry my sister!" Stating words found in the Qur'an, Abel/Hābīl calmly responded, "God accepts from the pious." (Ibn Kathīr)

The commentators also identify various ways in which Cain/Qābīl killed Abel/Hābīl, with some saying that it was with a piece of iron, while others maintaining that it was with a rock or through strangulation. After killing Abel/Hābīl, Cain/Qābīl did not know what to do next but he then saw two ravens fighting with each other to the point that one killed the other. The victor then dug a hole and buried the dead raven in it. This led Cain/Qābīl to do the same with the corpse of Abel/Hābīl. The literature also opens the story to larger themes of relationships between Muslims. For instance, in a well-known tradition the Prophet Muhammad states that if two Muslims face off with their swords in a fight to death, both the killer and the killed will be consigned to hell. His companions responded by asking "Oh Messenger of God, we understand this punishment for the killer, but why for the killed?" The Prophet responded, "He was intent on killing his brother." Thus, the story of Cain/Qābīl and Abel/Hābīl has become a lesson on how not to treat one's biological or spiritual sibling and how to avoid internal strife.

Questions/Issues

(1) What does it mean that Cain's/Qābīl's *nafs* helps him to kill his brother?
(2) Compare the actions and words of the characters in the Qur'an story with those of their biblical counterparts in Genesis 4:1–16. What are the most profound differences between the two versions, and what effect do they have on how you interpret them?
(3) Does the biblical story of the first murder have relevance for later audiences in the way the Qur'an one does?

Further Reading

Robert C. Gregg, Robert C. *Shared Stories, Rival Tellings: Early Encounters of Jews, Christians, and Muslims* (Oxford: Oxford University Press, 2015), pp. 75–108.

6

Children of Israel/Bānū Isrā'īl

Qur'an 3:93; 19:58; 7:104–5; 7:134, 137–38; 10:90, 93; 20:47, 80; 26:17, 22; 44:30; 45:16; 17:2; 32:23; 40:53; 2:40; 2:47, 83, 122; 5:12; 20:80; 5:70; 17:4–10; 2:246; 5:78; 61:6; 3:43; 5:72, 110; 43:59; 61:14

The Israelites are referred to as the Children of Israel/Bānū Isrā'īl approximately forty times in the Qur'an. This could be a way of tracing their lineage back to Jacob/Ya`qūb, who is identified twice in the text as Israel/Isrā'īl (3:93; 19:58). Each time the title occurs it designates a group of people in the distant past, and it is never used to describe Jews who were Muhammad's contemporaries, or who interacted with members of his community. In particular, the term Children of Israel/Bānū Isrā'īl is the Qur'an's preferred way of referring to Israelites who lived during biblical times.

More than one-half of the times it is found in the Qur'an the phrase Children of Israel/Bānū Isrā'īl refers to people who lived during Moses's/Mūsā's lifetime, especially those who escaped with him from Egypt and Pharaoh/Fir`awn during the Exodus. "Moses said, 'Oh Pharaoh, I am truly a messenger from the Lord of the worlds, and I am obliged to speak only the truth about God. I have brought you a clear sign from your Lord, so send out the Children of Israel with me'" (7:104–5; cf. 7:134, 137–38; 10:90, 93; 20:47, 80; 26:17, 22; 44:30).

A number of texts explain how the Children of Israel/Bānū Isrā'īl were the recipients of a book from God, which is identified elsewhere as the Torah that was given to Moses/Mūsā. "Truly, We gave the Children of Israel the book, the wisdom, and the prophetic office. We granted them good things, and We favored them over the worlds" (45:16; cf. 17:2; 32:23; 40:53). These gifts are part of the covenantal promise that God made with the Children of Israel/Bānū Isrā'īl. "Children of Israel, remember My blessing that I bestowed on you. Fulfill

My covenant, and I will fulfill your covenant. Fear Me alone" (2:40; cf. 2:47, 83, 122; 5:12; 20:80). Despite that special relationship they enjoyed with God, they were not able to live up to the terms of the covenant and went against the divine will. "We made a covenant with the Children of Israel, and We sent messengers to them. But whenever a messenger brought them what they did not want to hear, they called some of them liars and others of them they killed" (5:70; cf. 17:4–10). According to the Islamic view of prophetic history, the Israelites' inability to remain faithful and accept the divine message is what ultimately made necessary the sending of the Qur'an through Muhammad, the final prophet.

The Children of Israel/Bānū Isrā'īl are also mentioned in the Qur'an in relation to two other Hebrew Bible figures. In 2:246 they ask one of their prophets, commonly identified as Samuel in other Islamic sources, for a king so that they might fight in God's way. He is reluctant to grant their wish, and when he does so with the appointment of Saul/Ṭālūt only a few of them actually engage in fighting. Another verse pairs David/Dāwūd with Jesus/`Īsā as two prophets who criticized some of the Children of Israel/Bānū Isrā'īl for their lack of fidelity. "The Children of Israel who disbelieved were cursed by David and Jesus, son of Mary, because they disobeyed and transgressed" (5:78).

In six other passages the Children of Israel/Bānū Isrā'īl are mentioned in relation to Jesus/`Īsā, including two in which he addresses them using that title. One of the two is noteworthy because in it Jesus/`Īsā predicts the coming of Muhammad by using an alternate form of his name. "Children of Israel! I am truly God's messenger to you, attesting to the truth already in the Torah and announcing the good news of a messenger who will come after me whose name is Ahmad" (61:6; cf. 3:43; 5:72, 110; 43:59; 61:14). The three root letters of the Arabic name "Ahmad" are the same as those in "Muhammad," and the two names are considered to be variants of each other. This verse is one of the clearest examples of how prophets from the past are sometimes cited in the Qur'an in order to validate Muhammad's prophetic status.

Questions/Issues

(1) How does the Qur'an's understanding of the Children of Israel/Bānū Isrā'īl compare to how the Israelites are presented in the Bible?

(2) What is your reaction to Jesus's prediction of the coming of Muhammad in the Qur'an?

Further Reading

Rubin, Uri. *Between Bible and Qur'an: The Children of Israel and the Islamic Self-Image* (Princeton: Darwin Press, 1999), pp. 55–116.

7

Christians

Qur'an 5:46–47; 3:67; 2:62; 5:69; 2:113; 5:14; 2:120, 135; 2:111, 140; 5:18; 5:51; 5:55; 6:14; 5:17; 5:73; 4:171; 5:72, 116–18; 5:82–83; 9:31, 34; 57:27; 5:75, 116

Muhammad and the early Muslim community undoubtedly came into contact with Christianity and its followers, as seen in the fact that Christians are mentioned more than a dozen times in the text of the Qur'an. These and other passages sometimes make direct references to Christian beliefs and practices, which further points to Muslims' familiarity with the older religion. Other Islamic sources indicate that in the year 630 CE Muhammad established a pact with the Christians of Najran, which was an important city in southern Arabia that had its own bishop and was a popular pilgrimage site due to its shrine dedicated to martyrs from the area. This treaty, the first of its kind, guaranteed the Christians of Najran freedom of worship. Not much is known about Christianity in Arabia during this time period, but its followers were probably members of subgroups like the Nestorians, Jacobites, and Melkites, which traced their roots to Mesopotamia and Egypt and whose languages included Greek, Coptic, and Syriac.

One Qur'an passage describes Christians as "people of the Gospel" in a way that asserts the legitimacy of the Bible.

> We sent in their footsteps Jesus, son of Mary, confirming the Torah that had been sent before him. We gave him the Gospel, which contains guidance, light, and confirmation of the Torah sent before him—a guide and admonition for those who are mindful of God. So let the people of the Gospel judge by what God has revealed in it. Those who do not judge according to what God has sent down are transgressors. (5:46–47)

The Arabic word the Qur'an more commonly uses to refer to Christians is *naṣārā* (singular, *naṣrānī*), which is actually Syriac in origin and likely stems from Jesus's/'Īsā's association with the town of Nazareth. It is found fourteen times in the text and its singular form is present only in 3:67, where it is stated that Abraham/Ibrāhīm was neither a Jew nor a Christian. All fourteen occurrences of the term *naṣārā* also include a reference to Jews, and all but three of them are critical of both groups. Two of the three positive texts identify Jews and Christians as among those who will be rewarded by God (2:62; 5:69), while the other one privileges Christians over Jews. "You (Muhammad) will surely find that those most antagonistic toward the believers are the Jews and those who associate other gods with God. You will also find that the ones closest in affection toward believers are those who say, 'We are Christians.' That is because among them are priests and ascetics, and they are not boastful" (5:82a). The list of things that Christians (and Jews) are criticized for in the Qur'an includes bickering among themselves (2:113; 5:14), trying to lead Muslims astray (2:120, 135), and lying (2:111, 140; 5:18).

A Qur'an verse that has sometimes impaired relations between Muslims and Christians (and Jews) is found here. "Oh believers, do not take the Jews and Christians as allies. They are allies of one another, and anyone who takes them as allies is one of them. God does not guide an unjust people" (5:51). On occasion this passage has been cited as proof that the Qur'an counsels Muslims to avoid contact with Jews and Christians at all costs. This interpretation is based on a misunderstanding of the Arabic word *'awliyā'*, which is rendered here as "allies." Some (both Muslims and non-Muslims) maintain that the word should be translated as "friends," and that the Qur'an is therefore forbidding cordial and civil relations between Muslims and other monotheists. In both its singular (*walī*) and plural forms the term appears almost ninety times in the Qur'an, and among its possible meanings are "ally," "follower," "protector," "patron," "friend," and "legal guardian." Each time it is used it has to be read within its own literary and historical context in order to determine which meaning is most appropriate. This verse is from the fifth chapter of the Qur'an, which contains references to how Muslims were experiencing lack of respect and mistreatment from Jews, Christians, and others during Muhammad's time. It is therefore expressing caution about whom Muslims should associate with, rather than issuing a blanket condemnation of Christians and Jews. In other words, Muslims are being asked to join together and lean on one another for support and protection, a point that is clearly stated a few verses later in a passage that uses the same term. "Your allies are God, His messengers, and the believers—those who engage in prayer, pay alms, and bow down in worship" (5:55; cf. 6:14). To refer to God as a friend would go against Muslim views regarding the deity, and so the use of the term

ʾawliyāʾ here and several verses earlier in reference to Jews and Christians most likely conveys the sense of "allies" or "protectors."

A few Qur'an passages are critical of certain aspects of Christian faith that conflict with some of the basic tenets of Islamic theology. One of these is the idea of incarnation, the belief that Jesus/ʿĪsā was God in human form, which violates the Qur'an's prohibition against associating something from creation with the uncreated deity.

> Those who say, "God is the Messiah, the son of Mary," are truly unbelievers. Say (Muhammad), "Who would be able to stop God if He wanted to destroy the Messiah, son of Mary, his mother, and everyone else on earth?" God has authority over the heavens and earth and everything between. He creates whatever He wishes, and God has power over everything. (5:17; cf. 5:75)

The Christian belief in the Trinity, which teaches that God is three persons in one, also goes against Islamic doctrine and is considered to be an error in the Qur'an. "Those who say that God is the third of three are unbelievers. There is no god but the one God. If they do not desist in what they are saying, a painful punishment will come upon the unbelievers among them" (5:73; cf. 4:171). Elsewhere in the Qur'an, Jesus/ʿĪsā himself denies the Trinity and other claims his followers have falsely made about him (5:72, 116–18). Such passages can be difficult for Christians to read, but it is important for them to keep in mind that the Qur'an does not deny some of the central articles of their faith because of animosity or hatred toward them and their religion. It is rather due to Islam's radical monotheism (Arabic, *tawḥīd*), which rejects any ideas or concepts that might undermine or challenge the unity and oneness of God.

An expression of Christianity that is mentioned several times in the Qur'an is monasticism. Before Muhammad's lifetime communities of monks were well established in the areas surrounding Arabia, including in Egypt, Abyssinia (Ethiopia), Palestine, Syria, and Mesopotamia. Just prior to the emergence of Islam members of these monastic groups began to spread into the Arabian Peninsula, and there is some evidence of their presence in cities like Najran. Extra-Qur'anic Muslim sources speak of Muhammad's encounters with monks and Christian ascetics, and he would have been keenly aware of the important role that monasticism then played and continues to play in Christianity.

That key role is acknowledged in the Qur'an, where monks (*ruhbān*) are mentioned three times in the text. They are viewed positively in 5:82, a verse discussed above whose first half privileges Christians over Jews. The second half of that verse and the one that follows it go on to describe monks as pious people who are humbly receptive to God's word. This passage also contains the Qur'an's only reference to priests. "Among them are priests and ascetics who are not boastful, and when they listen to what is revealed to the Messenger you see their eyes overflowing with tears because they recognize the truth. They say, 'Our Lord, we believe, so count us among the witnesses'" (5:82b-83). The other two passages that mention monks, which are found only three verses apart, are less positive in their assessment of them. There they are presented as vain and self-centered individuals who are elevated above the other members of the Christian community and care only about their own needs.

> They take their scholars and their monks as lords, as well as the Messiah, the son of Mary. The only thing they were commanded was to serve only the one God—there is no god but He. Praise Him above what they associate with Him ... Oh believers, many scholars and monks vainly consume people's wealth and hinder them from God's path. Those who store up gold and silver, but do not spend it in God's way—give (Muhammad) them notice of a painful punishment. (9:31, 34)

The institution of monasticism is mentioned only in this instance, an ambiguous verse that can be interpreted in more than one way.

> We sent Our messengers in their footsteps, and then We sent Jesus, son of Mary. We gave him the gospel, and We put kindness and mercy in the hearts of those who follow him. But they invented monasticism (*rahbānīya*). We did not prescribe it for them—only that they desire God's pleasure, but they did not do so properly. We rewarded those who believed, but many of them were transgressors. (57:27)

The verse could be saying that monasticism was originally intended by God, but Christians distorted it and turned it into something else by introducing into it elements that were not part of God's will. It is also possible, however, that the text considers monasticism to be a purely human invention that was not part of the divine plan.

Despite the multiple references to Christianity in the Qur'an, it is uncertain exactly what form(s) of it Muhammad and his early community may have come into contact with. Christian beliefs and practices are sometimes described in the text in ways that do not reflect what have come to be viewed as mainstream or orthodox expressions of the faith. For example, one verse states that Jesus/'Īsā and his mother Mary/Maryam both ate food, suggesting that some believed the two of them were not in need of sustenance like normal people (5:75). The idea that Jesus only appeared to be human and did not have the same needs and urges as other people—a theological position known as Docetism—was held by some in the early centuries of Christianity, but it was eventually rejected as a heresy. A bit later in the same chapter, God asks Jesus/ʿĪsā if he ever taught his followers that he and his mother were gods (5:116). This passage suggests that there might have been Christians in Arabia who considered Mary/Maryam to be a member of the Trinity, a belief that falls outside the bounds of conventional Christian belief. The presence of texts like these raises important and provocative questions about what the Qur'an is referring to when it speaks of Christianity because, in some places at least, it is describing a religious system that most Christians would not recognize as their own. This inconsistency has important implications for Muslim–Christian relations in our own day.

Questions/Issues

(1) Is the view of Christians and Christianity in the Qur'an and other Islamic sources primarily a positive or negative one?
(2) How significant are Muslim and Christian disagreements over ideas like the incarnation and the Trinity?
(3) What are some of the implications for Christian–Muslim relations if the Qur'an and other Islamic sources sometimes refer to forms of Christianity that are not accepted today as mainstream?

Further Reading

McAuliffe, Jane Dammen. *Qur'ānic Christians: An Analysis of Classical and Modern Exegesis* (Cambridge: Cambridge University Press, 1991).
Ridgeon, Lloyd, ed., *Islamic Interpretations of Christianity* (New York: Routledge, 2001).

8

David/Dāwūd

Qur'an 2:251; 4:163; 17:55; 27:15; 21:79; 34:10–11; 21:80; 2:30; 38:16–28

David/Dāwūd is referred to by name sixteen times in the Qur'an, where he is given special abilities that are not all mentioned in the Bible. In addition, much of the biblical material related to his life is not found in the Islamic text, including traditions about his rise to power and his reign as king of Israel (1 Sam. 16–1 Kgs 2). A story shared by both texts is his slaying of Goliath/Jālūt (2:251; 1 Sam. 17), but the biblical version of the killing provides much more detail than the Qur'an's account. Both the Bible and the Qur'an associate David/Dāwūd with the Psalms, and the latter text says that God gave them to him (4:163; 17:55).

The Qur'an indicates that David/Dāwūd received other gifts and powers from God in addition to the book of Psalms. Although it describes very little of his time on the throne, the Qur'an states that the kingship was divinely bestowed upon him (2:251). The same verse also says that the deity gave him wisdom, and elsewhere it is claimed that he and his son Solomon/Sulaymān received knowledge from on high (27:15). A number of texts speak of David/Dāwūd (and Solomon/Sulaymān) in connection with birds and other elements of the natural world. One of them describes how he was compelled by God to sing the deity's praises. "We made the mountains and the birds, as well as David, glorify (Us). We did this" (21:79). Another passage says a similar thing and adds that God also taught David/Dāwūd how to work metal. "We granted David favor from Us. Oh mountains and birds, echo praises with him! We made iron soft for him" (34:10). Elsewhere, his skill in metalworking includes the ability to make armor and weapons (21:80; 34:11). Another thing that sets David/Dāwūd apart from virtually all others is that he and Adam/Ādam are the only two people in the

Qur'an who are given the title *khalīfah* (38:26; 2:30). This Arabic word, which is often translated as "successor" or "vice-regent," refers to someone who rules in place of or on behalf of someone else, and its use in reference to David/Dāwūd might be a way of indicating that his role as king is temporary at best because God is the only supreme sovereign.

The Qur'an's lengthiest passage on David/Dāwūd is found in 38:16–28, part of which describes a scene in which two men ask David/Dāwūd to resolve a dispute between them. The problem between them is that one of the men, who owns ninety-nine ewes, has taken the only ewe belonging to the other man. After criticizing the former for his actions, David/Dāwūd realizes that this is a test from God in response to an unspecified offense that he himself has committed. He repents and asks for forgiveness, and is then restored to God's good graces. While not identical to it, this scene has much in common with what is described in the Bible in 2 Samuel 12 when the Prophet Nathan confronts David/Dāwūd for the sins he committed in his affair with Bathsheba, the wife of Uriah the Hittite. Whatever its relationship to the biblical tradition might be, the episode is remarkable because it is a rare instance of a prophet seeking repentance in the Qur'an.

The account of David's/Dāwūd's life in "The Stories of the Prophets" provides the background on some of the traditions in the Qur'an and also includes other material not in the Islamic scripture. It relates a more detailed description of the killing of Goliath/Jālūt that is similar to the biblical version, and also mentions that David/Dāwūd married Michal the daughter of Saul/Ṭālūt. At one point Saul/Ṭālūt became jealous of David/Dāwūd and wanted to kill him, but it is reported that David/Dāwūd actually had the better opportunity to kill Saul/Ṭālūt while he was sleeping, but he chose not to do so. David's/Dāwūd's ability to speak the language of animals is attributed to the time he spent in the wilderness communing with nature.

According to "The Stories of the Prophets," David/Dāwūd did not profit financially from becoming king upon Saul's/Ṭālūt's death, but rather made a livelihood making and selling weapons through his ability to work metals. It is also reported that David/Dāwūd spent one-quarter of his day earning a living and resting, one-quarter in prayer, one-quarter listening to his people's concerns, and the final one-quarter giving sermons. Tradition says that David/Dāwūd died suddenly and was mourned by 4,000 priests and thousands of people, and the day was so hot that Solomon/Sulaymān ordered birds to create shade for the crowd (Ibn Kathīr).

Questions/Issues

(1) Are the similarities or the differences more apparent in the way the Bible and the Qur'an present David's/Dāwūd's character?
(2) Why does the Qur'an associate David/Dāwūd with birds and mountains?
(3) Compare the story of David/Dāwūd and the two disputants in Qur'an 28:16–28 with the one about him and the Prophet Nathan in 2 Samuel 12. What are the most significant similarities and differences between them?

Further Reading

Mohammed, Khaleel. *David in the Muslim Tradition: The Bathsheba Affair* (Lanham, MD: Lexington Books, 2014).

9

Disciples/Ḥawāriyyūn

Qur'an 3:52; 5:111–15; 61:14

The disciples of Jesus/`Īsā are mentioned four times in the Qur'an, where the Arabic term that refers to them is *ḥawāriyyūn*. In the New Testament the word "disciples" is used frequently and it can describe a large crowd of people who follow Jesus/`Īsā, or a smaller group like his twelve apostles. They do not have as prominent a role in the Qur'an, and the Islamic text does not identify any of the disciples by name or indicate how many of them there were. The word *ḥawāriyyūn* is grammatically plural, and it is never found in its singular form (*ḥawārī*) in the Qur'an. Various etymologies for the term have been proposed, with some of the most popular associating it with Arabic roots that describe someone who is pure or free of vice, one who is a faithful friend or assistant to another, and the act of bleaching or whitening clothing, The latter sense is the basis for the view of some commentators that the disciples of Jesus/`Īsā made their livelihoods working with garments rather than as being the fishermen described in the New Testament. More likely, the word comes from the Ethiopic term *ḥawārya*, which means "messenger," and is used for the disciples in translations of the New Testament in that language.

The first mention of the disciples in the Qur'an comes in a passage in which Jesus/`Īsā seeks to determine who will assist him in his role as God's prophet. "When Jesus sensed their unbelief, he said, 'Who are my helpers in the way of God?' The disciples said, 'We are God's helpers, and We have believed in God. Bear witness that we are submitters. Our Lord, we believe in what You have sent down, and we follow the messenger. Write our names down among those who bear witness'" (3:52–53). The New Testament passages that are closest to this one are those in the Gospels that describe the call of the disciples when Jesus/`Īsā first invites them to become his followers as seen, for example, in Mark 1:16–20. An interesting difference between the two, though, is that in the story in Mark, Jesus/ʿĪsā issues a command that they follow him, while in the Qur'an he poses a question to them. Another key difference is that all the focus in the New Testament text is on Jesus/ʿĪsā ("Follow me!"), but in the Qur'an it shifts to God as Jesus/ʿĪsā references the deity in his question and in their response the disciples both address and mention God. A wordplay is present in this passage in the original Arabic because the word for "helpers" (*anṣār*) and the term the Qur'an uses to refer to Christians (*naṣāra*) are quite close to one another. Another, somewhat abbreviated, description of this encounter between Jesus/ʿĪsā and his disciples is also found in 61:14.

The disciples are referred to twice in 5:111–15, where they ask Jesus/ʿĪsā to call on God to send down a table with food on it, from which they might eat and be assured of the truthfulness of his message. He does so, and then God responds by saying that anyone who disbelieves after the food-laden table has been given to them will be severely punished. The New Testament does not relate the same episode, but it recounts several events from the life of Jesus/ʿĪsā in which food figures prominently that some commentators have attempted to connect to this Qur'an text. For example, all four Gospels describe how Jesus/ʿĪsā was able to miraculously feed a large crowd of his followers, even though he had only some loaves of bread and a few fish (Mt. 14:13–21; Mk 6:32–44; Lk. 9:10b-17; Jn 6:1–15). Another New Testament scene that has been discussed in relation to this Qur'an one is the meal that Jesus/ʿĪsā had with his disciples the night before he died that is described in all the Gospels and is referred to by Christians as the Last Supper (Mt. 26:20–35; Mk 14:17–25; Lk. 22:14–38; Jn 13:1–17:26).

The disciples are presented as more spiritually mature in the Qur'an than they are in the Gospel, where their faith wavers at times. This might be due to the role they play in the Islamic text as examples for the people of Muhammad's time, who were asked to accept him as God's messenger. In two of the three passages in which they appear they refer to themselves as "submitters" (*muslimūn* in Arabic), and this is likely a way of making their relevance for the later Islamic community more obvious (3:52; 5:111).

The Islamic tradition builds on the Qur'anic narratives by making an explicit connection between the disciples of Jesus/ʿĪsā and the companions of Muhammad. Some scholars make this analogy in that both groups were composed of righteous individuals who studied, compiled, and transmitted their leader's message. However, the followers of the prophets, whether they were disciples or companions, were fallible and could have erred in their narrations. Thus, medieval Muslims differed from their Christian counterparts, who sometimes understood the disciples as divinely protected messengers of Jesus/ʿĪsā.

Questions/Issues

(1) What other points of similarity and difference can be noted in how the disciples of Jesus/`Īsā are described in the New Testament and the Qur'an?
(2) Compare in more detail the encounter Jesus/`Īsā has with his disciples in the Qur'an (3:52–53) with the call narrative Mark 1:16–20, in order to determine the different purposes and agendas of the two texts.
(3) Does it seem that the Qur'an passage that describes the table of food (5:111–15) is related to either the scenes in the New Testament about Jesus/`Īsā feeding a large crowd with very little food (Mt. 14:13–21; Mk 6:32–44; Lk. 9:10b-17; Jn 6:1–15), or the accounts of the last meal he had with his disciples (Mt. 26:20–35; Mk 14:17–25; Lk. 22:14–38; Jn 13:1–17:26)?

Further Reading

Mirza, Younus Y. "The Disciples as Companions: Ibn Taymiyya's and Ibn Qayyim's Evaluation of the Transmission of the Bible," *Medieval Encounters* (forthcoming).
Wheeler, Brannon M. *Prophets in the Quran: An Introduction to the Quran and Muslim Exegesis* (London: Continuum, 2002), pp. 308–10.

10

Elijah/Ilyās

Qur'an 6:85; 37:123–32

In the Qur'an, Elijah's name is written Ilyās, which is etymologically closer to its Christian form in Greek (Elias) than it is to its Jewish Hebrew form (Elijah). He is mentioned three times in the Qur'an, with the first being a listing of him as part of a group of four that includes Zachariah/Zakarīyā, John/Yaḥyā, and Jesus/ʿĪsā, who are all described as righteous (6:85). The other two references to Elijah/Ilyās are in the same passage (37:123–32), but the second time it is found with the different spelling Ilyāsīn. This anomalous form could be for rhyming purposes, because it enables the verse (v.130) to end with the same sound as that of the verses around it. The passage begins by referring to Elijah/Ilyās as a messenger (v.123), and it goes on to recount how he encouraged his people to avoid worship of false gods and maintain belief in the one true God as their ancestors before them had done. In keeping with the theme of the rejection of the prior prophets that is frequently mentioned in the Qur'an, and that likely is meant to validate the prophecy of Muhammad in the face of his own detractors, the people of Elijah/Ilyās call him a liar and refuse to accept his message. Nonetheless, he is vindicated in the end because future generations will wish him peace (v.130).

Elijah/Ilyās identifies the god whom his people wrongly follow as Baal (v.125), and this is the only reference in the Qur'an to the Canaanite deity who is often mentioned in the Hebrew Bible. In a famous scene in 1 Kings 18, Elijah/Ilyās successfully engages in a contest against 450 prophets of Baal in order to determine whose deity is superior to the other. The details of his biblical prophetic career mesh well with the purpose and message of the Qur'an, and the Hebrew Bible contains much more information about Elijah/Ilyās than the Islamic text does. This suggests that there were not many traditions about Elijah/Ilyās circulating in Arabia during Muhammad's lifetime.

Questions/Issues

(1) How else might the relatively sparse information about Elijah/Ilyās in the Qur'an as compared to the Bible be explained?
(2) Why could it be that the spelling of Elijah's/Ilyās's name in the Qur'an is closer to its Greek form than its Hebrew one?
(3) It has sometimes been argued that the variant spelling of Elijah's/Ilyās's name as Ilyāsīn in 37:130 is a plural form, and that the verse is actually calling for peace upon those who heed the message of Elijah/Ilyās rather than upon the prophet himself. Does this seem like a plausible interpretation?

Further Reading

Wheeler, Brannon M. *Prophets in the Quran: An Introduction to the Quran and Muslim Exegesis* (London: Continuum, 2002), pp. 243–47.

11

Elisha/Alyasa`

Qur'an 6:86; 38:48

Twice in the Qur'an, the name of Elisha/Alyasa` is found in lists that refer to prophets and other prominent figures of the past. In 6:86, he is mentioned along with Ishmael/Ismā`īl, Jonah/Yūnus, and Lot/Lūṭ as among those who are favored by God over other people. This verse concludes a listing of fourteen other important individuals who were chosen and guided on a "straight path" (6:83–87). The other reference to him is found in a shorter list in which he, Ishmael/Ismā`īl, and Dhū al-Kifl (who has been identified with various biblical figures) are remembered as being among the best people who have lived (38:48). Traditions related to the prophet Elisha/Alyasa` are recounted in the biblical books of 1 and 2 Kings (1 Kgs 19:16–21; 2 Kgs 2:1–10:27; 13:14–21), but none of these stories are in the Qur'an.

Further Reading

Wheeler, Brannon M. *Prophets in the Quran: An Introduction to the Quran and Muslim Exegesis* (London: Continuum, 2002), pp. 248–49.

12

Eve/Ḥawwāʾ

Qur'an 2:34–39; 7:19–25; 20:115–22

Adam's/Ādam's mate, who is unnamed in the Qur'an, is known as Eve/Ḥawwāʾ in other Islamic sources. She is alluded to in this verse, which describes her and Adam/Ādam as the ancestors from whom all human beings are descended. "Oh people, be mindful of your Lord, who created you from a single soul, and created from it its mate. From them spread out many men and women. So be mindful of God, by whom you request things of one another, and (be mindful of) your kinship relations. God watches over you" (4:1). This verse, as well as another one that says a similar thing (39:6), suggests that Eve/Ḥawwāʾ was made from some part of Adam/Ādam, but the Qur'an does not describe exactly how or when Eve/Ḥawwāʾ was created.

Several passages depict Eve/Ḥawwāʾ and Adam/Ādam in the garden, where they are deceived by Satan/Shayṭān and eat the fruit of a tree that God has forbidden them to eat (2:34–39; 7:19–25; 20:115–22). That disobedience leads to their expulsion from the garden and God sends them to earth, where they will die and from which they will eventually be brought forth. The description of their offense indicates that Eve/Ḥawwāʾ and Adam/Ādam act together and that they both eat from the tree at the same time. In the account in 7:19–25 the two of them acknowledge their mistake and ask for forgiveness and compassion from God. "They said, 'Our Lord, we have harmed ourselves. If you do not forgive us and have mercy on us, we shall surely be among the lost' " (7:23). Those two sentences, which she speaks with Adam/Ādam, are the only words that they utter in the Qur'an.

Similar to the biblical tradition, the commentators discuss the origins of Eve's/Ḥawwā's name as coming from "living" (*ḥayy*) because she was created from a living thing or Adam/Ādam. Moreover, while the Qur'an does not detail how Eve/Ḥawwāʾ was created, many of the commentators narrate that she was created from Adam's rib. In one popular story, Adam/Ādam was created and started to roam heaven by himself to the point that he got tired and fell asleep. When he woke up he found a woman sitting in front of him whom God had created from his rib. He then asked her, "Who are you?" to which she replied, "A woman." He further prodded, "Why were you created?" and she responds, "So that you may find rest with me." Similarly, the commenters draw from the biblical narrative to contend it was Eve's/Ḥawwā's fault for their eventual downfall since she is the one who encouraged Adam/Ādam to eat from the tree (Ibn Kathīr). Some further add that Eve's/Ḥawwā's sin led her and future women to bear the burden of pregnancy and the pain of childbirth (al-Ṭarafī). Modern scholars have stressed that the Qur'anic text (4:1) states that Eve/Ḥawwā' and humanity as a whole were created from "one soul," not from the rib of Adam/Ādam, and is thus open to more egalitarian readings.

Questions/Issues

(1) Does the way Eve/Ḥawwā' is presented in the Muslim sources provide any insight on how male/female relations are understood in Islam?
(2) How might we interpret the tradition that states that Eve/Ḥawwā' was formed from some part of Adam/Ādam?
(3) Does Eve's/Ḥawwā''s lack of a name in the Qur'an affect how you understand her character?

Further Reading

Bauer, Karen. *Gender Hierarchy in the Qur'ān: Medieval Interpretations, Modern Responses* (New York: Cambridge University Press, 2015).

Bronson, Catherine. "Eve in the Formative Period of Islamic Exegesis: Intertextual Boundaries and Hermeneutic Demarcations," in *Tafsīr and Islamic Intellectual History: Exploring the Boundaries of a Genre*, ed. Andreas Görke and Johanna Pink (Oxford: Oxford University Press in association with the Institute of Ismaili Studies, 2014), pp. 27–61.

Klar, Mariana. "Through the Lens of the Adam Narrative: A Re-consideration of *Sūrat al-Baqara*," *Journal of Qur'anic Studies* 17/2 (2015): 24–46.

Kvam, Kristen E., Schearing, Linda S. and Ziegler, Valarie H. *Eve and Adam: Jewish, Christian, and Muslim Readings on Genesis and Gender* (Bloomington: Indiana University Press, 1999), pp. 178–203.

Pregill, Michael. "Isrā'īliyyāt, Myth, and Pseudepigraphy: Wahb b. Munabbih and the Early Islamic Versions of the Fall of Adam and Eve," *Jerusalem Studies in Arabic and Islam* 34 (2008): 215–84.

Roded, Ruth. "Human Creation in the Hebrew Bible and the Qur'an—Feminist Exegesis," in *Religion Compass* 6/5 (2012), 277–86.

13

Ezra/`Uzayr

Qur'an 9:30–31

An individual named Ezra/`Uzayr is mentioned once in the Qur'an in a verse that is the only passage in the book that accuses Jews of engaging in *shirk*, the sin of associating something or someone in creation with the uncreated deity. "The Jews say, 'Ezra is the son of God,' and the Christians say, 'the Messiah is the son of God.' That is what they say with their mouths, imitating the words of those who disbelieved before them. May God fight against them—how perverse they are!" (9:30).

The identity of this person is not certain. There is a biblical character named Ezra/`Uzayr after whom one of the books of the Hebrew Bible is named, and this might be an allusion to him. He was an Israelite priest and scribe who lived in the fifth century BCE during the time of the exile in Babylon, and the Bible presents him as an important figure who led the effort to return to Judah after the exilic period. Because there is no evidence anywhere for it being an aspect of Jewish belief, the reference to Jewish worship of Ezra/`Uzayr as the son of God is obscure. It is likely that the passage reflects tension between the early Muslim community and some of the Jews of Medina, who did not accept Muhammad's legitimacy as a prophet.

The interpretation that interreligious conflict underlies the passage is supported by its criticism of Christian beliefs about Jesus and the content of the verse that follows it, which is critical of the role that Jewish and Christian leaders play in their communities. "They have taken their leaders, and monks, and the Messiah, son of Mary, as lords apart from God. They were not commanded anything except to worship the one God. There is no God but He. Praise be to Him above what they associate" (9:31). This verse states that leaders and monks, along with Jesus, were considered to be lords in a way that infringed on God's supremacy. The word for monks (*ruhbān*) refers to Christian ascetics. The meaning of the term translated as "leaders" (*aḥbār*) is a bit broader, since it refers to any learned Jew or Christian. The latter word might be used to designate Jewish leaders only, and the verse would therefore identify a particular group within both Judaism and Christianity. Regardless of how the terms are understood, the point of the passage is clear—members of the two communities were wrongly ascribing divinity to their leaders just as Jews were doing with Ezra/ʿUzayr, whoever he might have been.

Questions/Issues

(1) What might be the cause(s) of the Qur'an's critique of Jewish and Christian leaders?
(2) Is it possible that the Ezra/ʿUzayr mentioned in the Qur'an is the biblical Ezra?
(3) What impact might the presence of interreligious tension in Arabia have had on the content and message of the Qur'an?

Further Reading

Ayoub, Mahmoud. "ʿUzayr in the Qur'an and Muslim Tradition," in *Studies in Islamic and Judaic Traditions* ed. William M. Brinner and Stephen D. Ricks (Atlanta: Scholars Press, 1986), pp. 3–18.
Brown, Jonathan. "The Qur'an, the Jews and Ezra as the Son of God," (http://almadinainstitute.org/blog/the-quran-the-jews-and-ezra-as-the-son-of-god/).

14

Gabriel/Jibrīl

Qur'an 2:97; 16:102; 26:192–95; 40:51–53; 2:98

Gabriel/Jibrīl is the angel through whom the Prophet Muhammad received the revelation that comprises the Qur'an. This idea is conveyed here, one of three verses in which Gabriel/Jibrīl is mentioned by name in the text. "Whoever is an enemy of Gabriel—he was truly the one who brought it down into your heart with God's permission, as a confirmation of what had been before it and as guidance and good news for the believers" (2:97). The word "your" is grammatically masculine singular in Arabic, and so the common interpretation is that the text is addressed to Muhammad as an explanation of how the message came to him. Although the details are not spelled out in the verse, Muslim tradition teaches that the Qur'an is what has been brought down into his heart, and it confirms the Torah and Gospel that were sent to earlier prophets. Other Qur'an texts state that God's spirit is the means by which Muhammad received the divine revelation, so commentators have often equated Gabriel/Jibrīl with that spirit (16:102; 26:192–95; 40:51–53).

The verse that immediately follows contains another reference to Gabriel/Jibrīl and also mentions the angel Michael/Mīkāl. "Whoever is an enemy to God, His angels, His messengers, and Gabriel and Michael—truly, God is an enemy to the disbelievers" (2:98). While it is possible that the text could be suggesting that they should not be considered to be angels, it could also be that this is a way of saying that Michael/Mīkāl and Gabriel/Jibrīl enjoy a special status within the angelic ranks. The main point of the passage is that if one does not accept Michael/Mīkāl and Gabriel/Jibrīl, along with the messengers and the other angels, that person is not a true believer and therefore an enemy of God. The final mention of Gabriel/Jibrīl in the Qur'an is in 66:4, which is part of a cryptic passage that refers to an unidentified domestic dispute involving Muhammad and his wives. It urges two of his wives to repent of their mistake because Muhammad has God, Gabriel/Jibrīl, true believers, and the rest of the angels as his supporters.

There are three references to Gabriel/Jibrīl in biblical literature. He appears twice in the book of Daniel, where he interprets both a vision Daniel has (8:15–26) and the meaning of the phrase "seventy weeks" in the book of Jeremiah (9:20–27). In the New Testament, Gabriel/Jibrīl appears in the Gospel according to Luke as the angelic messenger who announces the births of John the Baptist (1:18–20) and Jesus (1:26–38).

Questions/Issues

(1) Are there similarities between how Gabriel/Jibrīl is presented in the Qur'an and the roles he plays in the Bible?

Further Reading

Völker, Katharina. "Two Accounts of Qur'anic Revelation," *Islam and Christian-Muslim Relations* 26/3 (2015), 271–86.

15

God

Qur'an 6:100; 53:19–22; 17:110; 19:18; 25:60; 36:52; 59:22; 78:37–38; 7:180; 20:8; 59:22–24; 7:11; 15:28–30; 55:27; 2:115; 28:88; 30:38; 76:9; 11:37; 23:27; 52:48; 54:13–14; 48:10a; 3:73; 5:64; 40:15; 9:129; 23:116; 43:82; 39:75; 40:7; 69:17; 96:1–2; 6:102; 13:16; 23:14; 39:62; 40:62; 59:24; 2:163; 5:73; 9:31; 18:110; 112:1–4; 6:19; 16:51; 17:111; 21:108; 37:4; 41:6; 4:48; 4:116; 5:72; 22:31; 7:23; 7:148–54; 3:3

Throughout the Qur'an, God is referred to with the Arabic term *allāh* (an abbreviated form of *al-ilāh*) that translates as "the deity." This was also the name of the chief god in the Arabian polytheistic religious system in the period prior to Islam. Some passages indicate that the Arabs ascribed offspring to Allah, and three of His daughters are mentioned by name in the text (6:100; 53:19–22). These beliefs are rejected in the Qur'an as examples of *shirk*, or association, which describes any attempt to violate or disrupt the unity of God (*tawḥīd* in Arabic) that is a defining quality of the deity.

Every chapter in the Qur'an except one begins with a phrase that calls attention to God. Sometimes referred to as the *basmala* based on its initial Arabic words, it states, "In the name of God, the merciful one, the compassionate one." It serves as an introduction or superscription for every chapter but the ninth one, and its absence there has been explained in a couple of ways. It might be that chapters 8 and 9 were originally one long composition that was divided up at a certain point in time. Another explanation suggests that chapter 9 does not start with the *basmala* because it makes frequent reference to the punishment that God will inflict on those who refuse to obey the divine will. As will be discussed below, the recurring presence of the *basmala* calls attention to other divine qualities that are consistently stressed in the Qur'an—the mercy and forgiveness of God. These traits are so closely identified with the deity that another title commonly used for God in the Qur'an is *al-raḥmān*, which translates as "the merciful one" in the *basmala* and is found nearly sixty times in the text. "Say, 'Call upon God or call upon the merciful one (*al-raḥmān*). Whatever name you call, the beautiful names are His'" (17:110; cf.19:18; 25:60; 36:52; 59:22; 78:37–38).

That verse's reference to the beautiful names is also mentioned elsewhere in the Qur'an (7:180; 20:8; 59:24), and these passages helped to give rise to a belief in Islam that God possesses ninety-nine names, each of which designates some divine characteristic or trait. Many of these names are found in the Qur'an, and they include such descriptors as "the Wise," "the Highest," "the All-Seeing," and "the Sustainer." The idea that God has ninety-nine names was sometimes controversial, especially early in Islamic history, because some have felt that it compromises the divine unity that is at the heart of Islamic theology. The names eventually came to be viewed as nothing more than qualities or attributes of the one God (*ṣifāt* in Arabic) that do not undermine the deity's essential oneness in any way, and many Muslims memorize the entire list of names or portions of it that they then recite with the use of prayer beads. God is completely transcendent and other in the Qur'an, but aspects of the divine nature are revealed to people through these attributes. In this way, the ninety-nine names play an important role in the Muslim view of God because they help to bridge the gap that exists between humanity and the deity due to God's transcendent nature by identifying aspects of that nature that people can relate to and understand. The divine names often appear in pairs in the Qur'an, and the longest list in the text contains a string of more than a dozen of them (59:22–24).

The way that God communicates in the Qur'an can also sometimes appear to challenge the divine unity, especially for Bible readers. Many texts have God speak using first person plural pronouns ("we," "us," "our"), and in some instances these forms appear in the same verse in which God is also referred to in the third person ("he," him," "his"). Such language does not indicate the presence of more than one deity, but is an example of what is sometimes called the divine "we." This is a more exalted form of speaking that is sometimes found in other texts, including the Bible. A biblical example of it can be seen in the creation story that is recounted in the first chapter of Genesis when God says, "Let us make humankind in our image" (Gen. 1:26). Plural forms in reference to the deity are also sometimes interpreted as reflecting ancient notions of a heavenly court where supernatural beings like angels are present who do God's will. This is found, for instance, in the Qur'an's creation story when God tells the angels to bow down before Adam/Ādam (7:11; 15:28–30).

Another issue regarding the deity's nature that has been controversial in the history of the interpretation of the Qur'an concerns the divine anthropomorphisms contained in the text. The references to God's face, eyes, and hands are similar to certain descriptions of the deity in the Bible, and it has been debated whether or not these terms refer to actual body parts possessed by God. An example of this can be seen in this verse, which reads, "The face of your Lord remains, possessing majesty and honor" (55:27; cf. 2:115; 28:88; 30:38; 76:9). Similarly, when Noah/Nūḥ is instructed by God to build the ark, he is told to do so "before Our eyes" (11:37; cf. 23:27; 52:48; 54:13–14). The divine hand is mentioned in a number of passages, as in this one. "Truly, those who pledge allegiance to you (Muhammad) pledge allegiance to God—God's hand is over their hands" (48:10a; cf. 3:73; 5:64). The Qur'an does not mention the divine body, ear, mouth, tongue, or foot, but there are often allusions to God hearing and speaking throughout the text. Also related to this issue are the frequent references in the Qur'an to the throne of God, as in this case where the deity is described as "the possessor of the throne" (40:15; cf. 9:129; 23:116; 43:82). Some passages appear to envision the throne as a physical object that is surrounded by angels (39:75) and carried about in heaven (40:7; 69:17).

Many Muslim commentators maintain that these and other examples of anthropomorphisms in the Qur'an should be read metaphorically and are not meant to be taken literally. Some have argued that the face of God refers to the divine essence, in contrast to the divine attributes that are described in the ninety-nine names. In the same way, when God's eyes are referred to, it is a way of calling attention to the guidance and protection that the deity exercises over the created world. These scholars believe that those passages that speak of the divine hand are actually employing a metaphor to acknowledge God's power over humanity and the world. Others have suggested that the anthropomorphisms should be read literally, but we have no way of knowing what they mean because the human experience and understanding of these terms is completely inadequate to comprehend what their significance is on the divine level. These and similar anomalies of the text of the Qur'an that are impossible for humans to understand have sometimes been interpreted through appeal to the Arabic phrase *bila kaif*, which means "without (knowing) how," as a way of claiming that some dimensions of God's existence remain a mystery to human beings.

God's role as the creator of all that exists is a central theme of the Qur'an. This is seen, for example, in what Islamic tradition maintains are the first words Muhammad received from God through the angel Gabriel/Jibrīl. "Recite in the name of your Lord, who created humanity from a clot of blood" (96:1–2). Some of the names of God call attention to the deity's role as creator, including *al-khāliq* ("the Creator") that comes from an Arabic root commonly used in the Qur'an to describe the divine creative activity. "That is God, your Lord. There is no God but He, the creator of all, so worship Him. He has authority over everything" (6:102; cf. 13:16; 23:14; 39:62; 40:62; 59:24). Another is *al-muṣawwir* ("the Fashioner"), which appears in 54:24 at the end of the list of more than a dozen titles describing God that was mentioned above. Other words from this Arabic root sometimes refer to activities like shaping and sculpting, so this title introduces an artistic dimension to God's creative role.

As already noted, the Qur'an teaches that there is no division within God and divine unity is a recurring theme in the text. "The One" is one of the ninety-nine names of God, and it has its basis in Islam's sacred text (2:163; 5:73; 9:31; 18:110). Among the countless passages that mention the divine unity, one of the most well known to Muslims is chapter 112, which is often found in mosques and on works of art. "Say, 'He is God the one, the eternal. He has begotten no one, nor was He begotten. He has no equal" (112:1–4; cf. 6:19; 16:51; 17:111; 21:108; 37:4; 41:6). The text's stress on divine oneness is the reason why *shirk*, or association, is considered to be the worst sin a person can commit. Any attempt to associate something from creation with the uncreated unity of God violates the essential nature of the deity and is the only offense that will not be forgiven. "Surely, God will not forgive having something associated with Him, but He will forgive anything short of that as He pleases. Whoever associates something with God has committed a grave sin" (4:48; cf. 4:116; 5:72; 22:31).

While highlighting the gravity of engaging in *shirk* and thereby violating God's unity, this verse also alludes to another divine trait that was mentioned above—that God is merciful toward humanity, and any sinner's offenses can be forgiven. The Qur'an explains how throughout history people have repeatedly failed to submit themselves to the divine will, but when they have expressed their remorse and have honestly repented they have been pardoned for what they have done. This is seen in the story of the very first couple, when Adam/Ādam and Eve/Hawwā' eat the forbidden fruit in the garden and God forgives them when they admit their mistake (7:23). God's mercy is also dramatically displayed in the Qur'an's telling of the golden calf episode (7:148–54; cf. Exod. 32) when, unlike in the biblical account, every person in the story experiences divine compassion and forgiveness. Divine mercy is not just mentioned in the *basmala* that opens every chapter in the Qur'an save one, but it is a theme that threads its way throughout the entirety of the text.

This may seem at odds with the opinion held by some non-Muslims that the Qur'an is a violent text in which God calls for the death and destruction of those who do not embrace Islam. While the Qur'an does permit bloodshed in places, it is important that these passages be interpreted in their unique historical contexts in the same way that most Jews and Christians read biblical texts that endorse violence. In the early years of the Islamic community, powerful individuals and groups were sometimes opposed to Muhammad and his message, and he and his followers sometimes had to resort to warfare in order to defend themselves and survive. Most of the more violent passages in the Qur'an are responding to that set of circumstances, and they are meant to provide instruction and hope to a nascent community that was struggling in the face of significant challenges and obstacles. Rather than expressing an attitude toward non-Muslims that is relevant for all times and places, these texts convey a message that was relevant for a particular moment in time in Arabia of the seventh century CE. While certain modern Muslim individuals and groups might argue that these verses are applicable today, it is important to understand them within their original historical contexts while considering the entirety of the Qur'an's message. In many other places, the Qur'an communicates a more positive view of how Muslims should interact with non-Muslims, and these are the passages that non-Muslims (and Muslims) should look to for guidance and instruction.

A final dimension of Islam's view of the deity that non-Muslims are often not aware of is that the God of the Qur'an and the God of the Bible are one and the same. This is seen in the Muslim view of revelation that maintains the one God has spoken to humanity throughout history. "He (God) has revealed to you the book (the Qur'an) in truth and in confirmation of what came earlier. He revealed to you the Torah, and the Gospel before this, as a guide for humanity" (3:3).

Some Jews and Christians have maintained that the God of Islam is not the God they follow, and they sometimes base this view on a selective reading of the Qur'an that considers the more violent passages in the text to represent its entire message. But that argument is not supported by the Qur'an itself, and it is not how Muslims understand things. For them, despite whatever differences that might exist among the groups, the same God's will has been revealed to Jews, Christians, and Muslims in the books they read.

Questions/Issues

(1) What is your reaction to the idea of the ninety-nine names of God?
(2) Which are more significant in your mind, the similarities or the differences in how the Qur'an and the Bible view God?
(3) Should Jews and Christians accept the notion that the God of the Bible and the God of the Qur'an are one and the same?

Further Reading

Lawrence, Bruce B. *Who is Allah?* (Chapel Hill: University of North Carolina Press, 2015).

16

Gog/Ya'jūj and Magog/Ma'jūj

Qur'an 21:95–97; 18:83–98

Gog/Ya'jūj and Magog/Ma'jūj are mentioned twice in the Qur'an, and it is generally believed that the terms identify two groups of violent and belligerent people who will make their presence known at the end of time. One passage claims that the people in any towns destroyed by God will not return to them until Gog/Ya'jūj and Magog/Ma'jūj are set loose and come swarming down from every hill. At that time, sinners will recognize their offenses and lament the coming destruction (21:95–97).

The other reference to Gog/Ya'jūj and Magog/Ma'jūj is found within a section of the Qur'an that treats the career of a figure identified as Dhū al-Qarnayn, which means "the one of the two horns," who is generally held to be Alexander the Great (18:83–98). The text explains how God established Dhū al-Qarnayn on the earth and gave him complete access to everything. He journeys to the far west, where he encounters a group of people whom God says he should either punish or help. He responds saying that he will punish the unbelievers among them and speak gently to the believers. He then travels to the place that is farthest east and sees a people who have no protection from the sun. Finally, he voyages to a place that is situated between two mountain ranges and meets a group of people who speak a different language that makes communication with him difficult. They ask Dhū al-Qarnayn to build a barrier that will separate them from Gog/Ya'jūj and Magog/Ma'jūj, who are stirring up trouble in the area, and he agrees to do so with their help. Using iron and molten brass, Dhū al-Qarnayn seals off the gap between the two mountain ranges, and thereby denies Gog/Ya'jūj and Magog/Ma'jūj entry into the other side until God tears down the barrier on the last day.

In the Bible, Gog/Ya'jūj and Magog/Ma'jūj are described in Ezekiel 38–39 as a menacing force that will rise up against Israel in the final days and be defeated by God in an eschatological battle. In those chapters Gog/Ya'jūj is presented as a military leader, and Magog/Ma'jūj is the land he is from. In the New Testament book of Revelation, which contains the only other reference to Gog/Ya'jūj and Magog/Ma'jūj in biblical literature, things are somewhat different (20:7–10). There, they are described as two nations with large populations that are deceived by Satan into attacking the city of Jerusalem. They are destroyed when fire comes down from the heavens to consume them, and Satan is cast into a lake of fire and sulfur for eternity.

The identification of Dhū al-Qarnayn with Alexander the Great is supported by a Syriac Christian text known as "The Legend of Alexander" from the sixth century CE. It is one of the earliest of the apocalyptic versions of Alexander's life, and it contains some intriguing parallels with the Qur'an passage about Dhū al-Qarnayn. It describes in part how Alexander builds a gate in the north between two mountains to hold back Gog/Ya'jūj and Magog/Ma'jūj until some future period in time. The account is based on other sources, some of them biblical, that vary in their details, but there is no denying that there is a close connection between the Syriac text and the Qur'an passage that describes Dhū al-Qarnayn.

Questions/Issues

(1) Does the reference to Alexander the Great in the Qur'an seem unusual?
(2) How might the similarities between the story of Dhū al-Qarnayn in the Qu'ran and the Syriac Christian text "The Legend of Alexander" be explained?
(3) What are some of the similarities and differences between how Gog/Ya'jūj and Magog/Ma'jūj are presented in the Qur'an and the Bible?

Further Reading

van Donzel, Emeri and Schmidt, Andrea. *Gog and Magog in Early Christian and Islamic Sources: Sallam's Quest for Alexander's Wall* (Leiden: Brill, 2010).

17

Goliath/Jālūt

Qur'an 2:249–51

Goliath/Jālūt is mentioned by name three times in the Qur'an, in a passage that describes him as an enemy of the Israelites who is defeated and put to death by David/ Dāwūd. As they make their way to battle, the Israelite forces under Saul/ Ṭālūt are reduced in size through a test God has them undergo at a river. This is similar to what takes place in a biblical scene described in Judges 7:4–7 involving Gideon. In both cases, the manner in which the men drink from the river determines who will remain a member of the army. According to the Qur'an, as they prepare to engage the enemy some of the Israelites express fear that they will be defeated, while others are confident that God will enable them to emerge victorious. Those in the latter group prove to be correct as the text says, "They (the Israelites) vanquished them with God's permission" (v.251). This is an example of how the Qur'an sometimes presents stories about important figures of the past in ways that speak to the circumstances of Muhammad's life. In this case, the faith and trust in God exhibited by the Israelites is meant to be an example for the early Islamic community, which often felt threatened by enemies that outnumbered them considerably.

The two references to Goliath/Jālūt "and his army" in the story (vv.249, 250) suggest that he may have been a military leader for his people, who remain unidentified in the Qur'an. This is different from the Bible, where he and they are described as Philistines (1 Sam. 17). In the Islamic text Goliath's/Jālūt's people are identified in theological, not in geographic or ethnic, terms when the Israelites refer to them as "unbelievers" (v.250). The details of how David/ Dāwūd slays Goliath/Jālūt are not given in the Qur'an, but after reporting his death the final words of the passage make it clear that the world has become a better place without him. "If God did not remove some by means of others, the earth would be completely corrupt" (v. 251).

Questions/Issues

(1) Compare Goliath's/Jālūt's character in the Qur'an to the way he is presented in the Bible in 1 Samuel 17.

(2) Is there a stronger theological element in the Qur'an's story of Goliath/ Jālūt than there is in the Bible?

Further Reading

Lindsay, James E. "Goliath," in *Encyclopaedia of the Qur'ān*, ed. Jane Dammen McAuliffe (Leiden: Brill, 2002).

18

Haman/Hāmān

Qur'an 28:6, 8, 38; 40:36–37; 40:23–24; 29:39–40

Haman/Hāmān is a member of the court of Pharaoh/Fir`awn who is named six times in the Qur'an, usually in texts that mention both the Egyptian ruler and Moses/Mūsā. He functions as a counselor or advisor for Pharaoh/Fir`awn, and two references to their armies suggest there might be a military dimension to his office. One verse states that the establishment of the Israelites in Egypt will make Pharaoh/Fir`awn, Haman/Hāmān, and their forces fearful (28:6), and the other describes them as evil people. "Truly, Pharaoh, Haman, and their legions were sinners" (28:8).

Mention is made of Haman/Hāmān in two texts that contain possible allusions to the biblical Tower of Babel story (Gen. 9:1–11) because of their references to clay bricks, a tower, and the desire to climb up the tower in order to see God. "Pharaoh said, 'Oh nobles, I know of no other god for you except myself. Oh Haman, burn for me clay (bricks) and make for me a tower so that I might ascend to the god of Moses, for I think he is a liar" (28:38). The other passage is similar, except that Pharaoh/Fir`awn does not mention clay bricks and the Arabic word *asbāb* identifies the means by which he will reach heaven (40:36–37). This term is found elsewhere in the Qur'an, where it can mean "rope" or "way" (2:166; 18:84, 85, 89, 92; 22:15; 38:10).

Two other passages include Korah/Qārūn along with Pharaoh/Fir`awn and Haman/Hāmān as enemies of the Israelites. In one, the three of them accuse Moses/Mūsā of being a liar and a magician, and they issue a command that calls for the death of the sons of all the people who follow Moses's/Mūsā's God (40:23–24). This is similar to an earlier command that was given at the time when Moses/Mūsā was born. The other text explains in a similar way how the three refused to accept Moses/Mūsā, but it goes on to describe the way they each met their demise when Korah/Qārūn was swallowed by the earth, and Pharaoh/Fir`awn and Haman/Hāmān were drowned in the sea (29:39–40).

The identity of Haman/Hāmān has been the subject of some debate by commentators. A figure with the same name is found in the biblical book of Esther (3:1–6; 7:6–10), where he is a minister of the Persian king Ahasuerus, and an enemy of the Jews. Some scholars, mostly non-Muslim, have proposed a connection between this biblical character and the Haman/Hāmān mentioned in the Qur'an, but this idea has been rejected by Muslim commentators. Another theory suggests that Haman/Hāmān is not a personal name but a title that refers to the high priest of the Egyptian god Amun, who was a prominent official in Pharaoh's court.

Questions/Issues

(1) With what qualities and traits is the character of Haman/Hāmān most closely identified in the Qur'an?
(2) How does his character in the Qur'an compare to the one with the same name in the Bible's book of Esther?
(3) What should be made of the connections with the biblical Tower of Babel story present in some Qur'an passages that mention Haman/Hāmān?

Further Reading

Syed, Sher M. "Hāmān in the Light of the Qur'an," *Hamdard Islamicus* 4/7 (1984), 83–92.

19

Iblīs

Qur'an 2:34–39; 7:10–25; 15:28–48; 17:61–65; 18:50; 20:115–23; 38:67–84; 55:15; 26:95; 34:15–21

Iblīs is a fallen angel in the Qur'an, whose name appears eleven times in the text. Muslim commentators and lexicographers have sometimes proposed an origin for the name from an Arabic verb (*ublisa*) that means "to be in a state of complete despair," but it is in all likelihood an Arabicization of the Greek word *diabolos* from which the English term "devil" is derived.

Most of the references to him in the Qur'an are found in stories about the creation of Adam/Ādam that describe how Iblīs refused to bow down to him at God's command (2:34–39; 7:10–18; 15:28–48; 17:61–65; 18:50; 20:115–23; 38:67–84). Because of this act of disobedience Iblīs is expelled from paradise, but he vows that he will continue to be humanity's enemy. The reason why he refuses to bow before Adam/Ādam is his pride and sense of superiority that places him above God's human creation. "God asked, 'What prevented you from prostrating when I commanded you?' He replied, 'I am better than he. You created me of fire, but You created him of clay' " (7:12; cf. 15:33; 17:61; 38:76). In several versions of the story, Iblīs asks mercy of God for his offense and it is granted to him, but he nonetheless insists that he will continue to deceive humanity at every opportunity.

> God said, "Go down from here! You are not to be proud here. Leave! You are now among the despised ones." He replied, "Grant to me a delay until the day that they are raised up." He said, "You are reprieved." He declared, "Because you have caused me to err, I will surely lie in wait for them on your straight path. Then I will come upon them from the front and from behind, upon their right side and upon their left side. You will not find the majority of them thankful." (7:14–17; cf. 15:36–40; 17:62–64; 38:79–84)

There is some ambiguity in the Qur'an regarding Iblīs' precise identity. On one hand, he is presented as an angel because most of the scenes with Adam/

Ādam report that God orders all of the angels to prostrate and only Iblīs does not do so, implying that he is one of them (2:34; 7:11; 15:30–31; 17:61; 16:50; 38:73–74). In some cases, though, his character changes to that of Satan/Shayṭān as he deceives the first couple into eating the fruit of the tree that God has prohibited from them (2:34–36; 7:11–20; 20:115–20). Things are further complicated by a verse that indicates Iblīs is one of the jinn and that he has offspring, both of which would exclude him from the ranks of the angels (18:50). At the same time, though, this would explain his comment cited above that he was created from fire because that is the substance the Qur'an says that the jinn were made from (55:15). The text could be suggesting that Iblīs was originally created as an angel, but, due to his disobedience, he lost that status and became one of the jinn. His identification as Satan/Shayṭān might be due to a similar transformation. Prior to his refusal to bow down to the first human he was known as Iblīs, but after refusing to submit to the divine will he became Satan/Shayṭān. This interpretation is supported by Satan's/Shayṭān's role elsewhere in the Qur'an, where he is consistently presented as a figure who tempts people rather than one who is proud or disobedient.

Two other passages that refer to Iblīs do not recount the scene with Adam/Ādam, but they have connections to it because they illustrate how his promise to harm humanity was realized. One alludes to the forces of Iblīs who are punished in hell for their sins (26:95), and the other describes how Iblīs was able to deceive a group of people in a way that led to their own destruction (34:15–21). There is no exact equivalent to the figure of Iblīs in the Bible, but the devil is mentioned frequently in the New Testament. A tradition about the angels bowing down to Adam/Ādam and the devil refusing to join them is found in some Jewish and Christian texts like "The Life of Adam and Eve," which was written prior to the fifth century CE.

"The Stories of the Prophets" literature primarily discusses Iblīs in the context of the creation story, specifically his debate with God and his deception of Adam/Ādam and Eve/Ḥawwā'. Some begin by speaking about Iblīs' name, such as that it used to be al-Ḥārith and he once served as one of the guards of paradise. Others say that he used to be one of the most knowledgeable and hard-working angels, a status that eventually led him to become arrogant (al-Ṭarafī). His arrogance is best exemplified in his refusal to prostrate to Adam/Ādam and his statement to God "You created me from fire, and you created him from clay." The commentators refute Iblīs' claim by pointing out that in fact clay is more beneficial than fire because of its usefulness, longevity, and predictability (Ibn Kathīr).

Drawing on the biblical tradition, many of the commentators imagine Iblīs to be a serpent who tempted Adam/Ādam and Eve/Ḥawwā' to sin. The scholars speak about how Iblīs sought to enter paradise to whisper to Adam/Ādam and Eve/Ḥawwā' in order to convince them to eat from the forbidden tree. However, the guards prevented him from entering so he appealed to his friend the serpent, who had four legs and was one of the guards of paradise. The serpent allowed Iblīs to enter into his mouth, and the serpent then passed by the guards of paradise without any difficulty. When Iblīs entered paradise, he began to envy Adam/Ādam to the point that he said, "I have been worshiping God for a thousand years and he did not allow me to enter Paradise, yet God created this creature (Adam/Ādam) just now and allowed him to enter into paradise!" Iblīs was then able to approach Adam/Ādam and Eve/Ḥawwā', and he then began to cry and moan. Hearing those cries, Adam/Ādam and Eve/Ḥawwā' became saddened and asked Iblīs why he was crying. He responded that he wept because of the thought that they would both die and thus leave the blessings and honors of paradise. Iblīs was then able to trick them into eating from the forbidden tree by swearing by God that they would become angels and live eternally (al-Tha'labī). Thus, "The Stories of the Prophets" literature presents Iblīs as a disgruntled creation of God, whose arrogance leads him to envy Adam/Ādam and eventually trick him into sin.

Questions/Issues

(1) Are there any other ways of explaining why Iblīs is referred to as Satan/Shayṭān in some Qur'an passages?
(2) What does Iblīs' role in the Qur'an suggest about the text's view of the nature and cause of human sin and error?
(3) Should the figure of Iblīs be equated with the devil?

Further Reading

Awn, Peter. *Satan's Tragedy and Redemption: Iblīs in Sufi Psychology* (Leiden: E. J. Brill, 1983)

Bodman, Whitney S. *The Poetics of Iblīs: Narrative Theology in the Qur'an* (Cambridge, MA: Harvard University Press, 2011).

20

Isaac/Isḥāq

Qur'an 2:133, 136, 140; 3:84; 4:163; 6:84; 11:71–73; 12:6, 38; 14:39; 15:54–55; 19:49; 29:27; 37:101–13; 38:25

Isaac/Isḥāq is a son of Abraham/Ibrāhīm, who is referred to by name seventeen times in the Qur'an. He is a relatively minor character in the text, and he is mentioned primarily in lists of important figures from the past and in passages that describe how God gave him to Abraham/Ibrāhīm and his wife. He is identified as a prophet twice in the text (19:49; 37:112).

Isaac's/Isḥāq's name is present in various lists that identify ancient prophets and other important individuals from the past. In one passage, he is mentioned along with Abraham/Ibrāhīm and Ishmael/Ismāʿīl (2:133). Whenever he and Ishmael/Ismāʿīl are in the same list, the latter's name always appears first (2:136, 140; 3:84; 4:163). In other passages, Isaac/Isḥāq is mentioned between the names of Abraham/Ibrāhīm and Jacob/Yaʿqūb (2:136, 140; 38:25), sometimes followed by references to the tribes of Israel and other prophets (3:84; 4:163). Isaac/Isḥāq is referred to twice in the Joseph/Yūsuf story that is related in chapter 12 of the Qur'an. Early in the chapter, Joseph's/Yūsuf's father Jacob/Yaʿqūb instructs his son not to tell his brothers about a dream he has had, and he reminds him of the special relationship their family has with God. "Thus, your Lord will choose you, teach you how to interpret events, and confer His favor upon you and upon the family of Jacob, just as He conferred it earlier upon your two ancestors Abraham and Isaac" (12:6). When Joseph/Yūsuf is imprisoned later in the story, he echoes his father's words when he begins a speech to two fellow prisoners with the words, "I follow the religion of my fathers Abraham, Isaac, and Jacob" (12:38).

The Qur'an indicates that Abraham/Ibrāhīm was already advanced in years when his sons were born. "Praise be to God who has given to me, in spite of old age, Ishmael and Isaac" (14:39). The account of the visit that God's messengers made to Abraham/Ibrāhīm to announce the birth of his son is the only time Isaac's/Isḥāq's name appears twice in the same verse in the Qur'an. "His wife, standing by, laughed when We gave her the good news of Isaac and, after Isaac, Jacob" (11:71). Isaac/Isḥāq and Jacob/Ya`qūb are linked in a similar way elsewhere, where the reader could get the impression that they are brothers rather than father and son, but it is also possible to read these texts as identifying the generations that come after Abraham/Ibrāhīm. "We gave him (Abraham/Ibrāhīm) Isaac and Jacob, and We granted his offspring the prophetic office and the Book" (29:27; cf. 6:84; 19:49). The Qur'an's only explicit reference to the offspring of both Abraham/Ibrāhīm and Isaac/Isḥāq is less positive in that it indicates that some of them have failed to live up to the high moral standards that were set by their two illustrious ancestors. "We gave him the good news of Isaac, a prophet from among the righteous. We blessed him and Isaac, and some of their descendants are good people while other are clearly evildoers" (37:112–13).

Within the Stories of Prophets and exegetical literature, the birth of Isaac/Isḥāq is given prominence since it is mentioned several times in the Qur'anic text. The literature details how the angels in the form of handsome men—identified as Gabriel/Jibrīl, Michael/Mīkāl, and Isrāfīl by Ibn Kathīr—came to Abraham's/Ibrāhīm's and Sarah's house as guests. This led the hosts to prepare a fatted calf for them from the best of their cows (al-Thaʿlabī and Ibn Kathīr). However, when they brought the cooked calf and presented it to them, the guests displayed no interest in eating. Abraham/Ibrāhīm then became frightened, but the angels quickly reassured him by saying that he should not be scared as they were travelling to destroy the people of Lot/Lūṭ. The angels then gave Sarah the glad tidings of Isaac/Isḥāq, leading her to scream and slap her face in amazement and exclaim, "Alas for me! How am I to bear a child when I am an old woman, and my husband here is an old man? That would be a strange thing!" (11:72). The angels responded by asking, "Are you astonished at what God ordains? The grace of God and His blessings be upon you, people of this house! For He is worthy of all praise and glory" (11:73). Similarly, Abraham/Ibrāhīm was startled by the good news of the birth of Isaac/Isḥāq, and initially he had difficulty accepting the glad tidings. Once Abraham/Ibrāhīm hears of it he asks, "How can you give me such news when old age has come to me? What sort of news is this?" (15:54). The angels reply by stating, "We have told you the truth, so do not despair" (15:55), which leads Abraham/Ibrāhīm to accept God's order and declare that only the misguided lose hope in God's mercy.

Some Muslim scholars try to reconcile the Qur'anic story with the biblical account by noting that the "People of the Book" say that the angels actually ate the food that was given to them (Ibn Kathīr). Another report narrates that it appeared that they were eating, but the food simply vanished into thin air. This last tradition is more consistent with the Qur'an, where the angels do not show any interest in eating and do not seem to eat the food presented to them.

Isaac/Isḥāq further appears in the Islamic sources in the context of a discussion over which of his sons was nearly sacrificed by Abraham/Ibrāhīm. Even though the sacrificial son is not explicitly named in the Qur'anic text, early exegetes believed the son to be Isaac/Isḥāq based on a philological and intertextual reading of the Qur'an (al-Ṭabarī). For instance, the Qur'an uses the phrase "We gave the good news" to describe both the birth of Isaac/Isḥāq in 11:71 and the son nearly sacrificed in 37:101. According to this interpretation, since the same phrase is used the son must be the same. Moreover, after the story of the near sacrifice concludes, the Qur'an explicitly mentions Isaac/Isḥāq in 37:112 as being given the "good news" of prophecy. For these early exegetes, Isaac/Isḥāq was rewarded with the gift of prophecy because he passed the test of the sacrifice.

Questions/Issues

(1) What is Isaac's/Isḥāq's main role in the Qur'an?
(2) How should the reference to the evil nature of some of Isaac's/Isḥāq's descendants be interpreted?
(3) How is Islam's presentation of Isaac/Isḥāq similar to and different from his biblical counterpart?
(4) What do you think of Muslim scholars' attempts to reconcile the Qur'anic narrative with the biblical one?

Further Reading

Firestone, Reuven. "Abraham's Son as the Intended Sacrifice (al-Dhabīh, Qur'ān 37:99–113): Issues in Qur'ānic Exegesis," *Journal of Semitic Studies* 34/1 (1989): 95–131.

Firestone, Reuven. *Journeys in Holy Lands. The Evolution of the Abraham-Ishmael Legends in Islamic Exegesis* (Albany, NY: State University of New York Press, 1990).

Firestone, Reuven. "Comparative Studies in Bible and Qur'ān: A Fresh Look at Genesis 22 in Light of Sura 37," in *Judaism and Islam: Boundaries, Communication and*

Interaction: Essays in Honor of William M. Brinner, ed. Benjamin H. Hary, John L. Hayes and Fred Astren (Leiden: Brill, 2000), pp. 169–84.

Savant, Sarah Bowen. "Isaac as the Persians' Ishmael: Pride in the Pre-Islamic Past in Ninth and Tenth-century Islam," *Comparative Islamic Studies* 2/1 (2006): 5–25.

Wheeler, Brannon M. *Prophets in the Quran: An Introduction to the Quran and Muslim Exegesis* (London: Continuum, 2002), pp. 112–17.

21

Ishmael/Ismā`īl

Qur'an 14:39; 2:136, 140; 3:84; 4:163;19:54; 2:133; 6:86; 21:85; 38:48; 2:125, 127–29; 14:37; 37:101–12

Ishmael/Ismā`īl is a son of Abraham/Ibrāhīm, who is referred to by name twelve times in the Qur'an. Almost all of the references to him in the text are in lists that include him among prophets and prominent individuals of the past. He and Isaac/Isḥāq are born to Abraham/Ibrāhīm in his old age (14:39), but the Qur'an never explicitly identifies them as brothers. Whenever Ishmael/Ismā`īl and Isaac/Isḥāq are found together in the same list, the former's name always appears first (2:136, 140; 3:84; 4:163). The only verse that mentions Ishmael/Ismā`īl by himself offers a praiseworthy assessment of him and assigns him two lofty titles. "Remember Ishmael in the book. He was indeed true to the promise, and he was a messenger and prophet" (19:54).

One of the lists in which Ishmael's/Ismā`īl's name is found alongside those of Abraham/Ibrāhīm and Isaac/Isḥāq refers to only the three of them (2:133), while several others also include Jacob/Ya`qūb and the tribes of Israel (2:136, 140; 3:84). In one verse, the latter list is expanded to include references to other important individuals. "We have indeed inspired you (Muhammad) as We inspired Noah and the prophets after him—as We inspired Abraham, Ishmael, Isaac, Jacob, the tribes, Jesus, Job, Jonah, Aaron, and Solomon. We gave David the Psalms" (4:163). As this verse indicates, such lists often serve the purpose of validating Muhammad's status as a prophet in the face of doubts from his adversaries. In a few cases, Ishmael's/Ismā`īl's name is not found with those of Abraham/Ibrāhīm and Isaac/Isḥāq, but is listed with Elisa/Alyasa`, Jonah/Yūnus, Lot/Lūṭ, Idrīs (likely Ezra), and a figure known as Dhū al-Kifl, who some have identified as Ezekiel or Elijah (6:86; 21:85; 38:48).

The Qur'an associates Abraham/Ibrāhīm and Ishmael/Ismā`īl with the Ka`ba in Mecca, the shrine and pilgrimage site that predates Islam, toward which

Muslims face five times each day when they pray. "We made an agreement with Abraham and Ishmael to purify My house for those who circumambulate, the devout, and those who bow and prostrate" (2:125b). The two of them built the structure and then uttered a prayer comprised of three petitions: (1) that God be pleased with their work; (2) that God make them and their community submitters (*muslimūn*); and (3) that God raise up a messenger from within their community who will bring them God's word. The last petition is an allusion to Muhammad, and is a further illustration of how the careers of earlier prophets are sometimes mentioned in the Qur'an to legitimate Muhammad's prophetic status.

> Abraham and Ismael raised the foundations of the house saying, "Our Lord, accept it from us. You are the one who hears, the one who knows. Our Lord, make us submissive to You, and make of our offspring a community submissive to You. Show us our forms of worship and mercifully turn to us, for You are the often-returning one, the merciful one. Our Lord, send forth to them a messenger from among them who will recite Your revelations to them and teach them the book and wisdom so that he may purify them. You are truly the one who is mighty, the one who is wise. (2:127–29)

Ishmael/Ismā`īl plays a key role within "The Stories of the Prophets" and Islamic exegetical literature as the progenitor of Muhammad, the son nearly sacrificed by Abraham/Ibrāhīm, and the builder of the Ka'ba. Similar to what is found in the biblical narrative (Gen. 16), the birth of Ishmael/Ismā`īl is discussed in the context of Sarah being unable to have a child with Abraham/Ibrāhīm. She then gives her slave girl Hagar (who is not mentioned in the Qur'an) to Abraham/Ibrāhīm, and Hagar soon becomes pregnant. Sarah immediately becomes jealous, which leads her to complain to Abraham/Ibrāhīm to the point that Hagar becomes afraid and runs away. As she flees, an angel appears to Hagar and urges her not to fear, since God will give her much good through a son who will be named Ishmael/Ismā`īl. For many Muslim scholars these glad tidings extend all the way to Muhammad, who is seen as part of the blessing given to Hagar. Some include the detail that when Ishmael/Ismā`īl was born, he was like a moon that reflected the light of Muhammad in his face (al-Kisā'ī).

"The Stories of the Prophets" relate that after Hagar gave birth to Ishmael/Ismā`īl, Sarah's jealousy intensified to the point that she ordered Abraham/Ibrāhīm to take Hagar away, so she would not have to see her face (Ibn Kathīr). Abraham/Ibrāhīm then took Hagar and Ishmael/Ismā`īl to an area traditionally associated with modern-day Mecca. When they reached Mecca and Abraham/Ibrāhīm turned back for home, Hagar grabbed his robe and cried, "Oh Abraham, where are you going? Are you leaving us here, where there is not enough (to provide for us)?" Despite her persistence, he did not respond until she finally asked, "Did God order you to do this?" He then answered "Yes," which caused Hagar to declare, "Then God will not forsake us!"

Some sources explain that after Abraham/Ibrāhīm departed and could no longer see Hagar and Ishmael/Ismāʿīl, he recited a verse found in the Qur'an that asks God to support his family in order that they might continue to worship. "Our Lord, I have established some of my offspring in an uncultivated valley, close to Your Sacred House, so that they may keep up prayer. Make people's hearts turn to them, and provide them with produce, so that they may be thankful" (14:37). Soon after this, Ishmael/Ismāʿīl became thirsty and began to squirm. Seeing her child in distress, Hagar left for the nearest mountain, named Ṣafā, and stood upon it hoping to find someone who might assist her. She then moved from Ṣafā to another mountain named Marwa, and once again stood upon it searching for help. Hagar went back and forth between the mountains seven times, occasionally running between them. After the seventh time, when she returned to Marwa, she turned and saw an angel in the place where the well of Zamzam is located today. The angel hit the earth (some sources say he did so with his wing) until water began to appear (Ibn Kathīr). As the water began to gush out, birds started to circle over the well, causing some Arab tribes to become aware of the water. When they approached the well, they found Hagar and Ishmael/Ismāʿīl sitting beside it. They asked Hagar's permission for them to reside near the water source, and she responded, "Yes, but you do not have any (exclusive) right to our water." The tribe agreed and Ishmael then grew up among the Arabs, marrying one of their daughters and learning Arabic (al-Thaʿlabī). When Ishmael/Ismāʿīl became older, Abraham/Ibrāhīm eventually returned and together they built the Kaʿba, as recorded in the Qur'an.

Some of these traditions from "The Stories of the Prophets" that are associated with Hagar are connected to rituals that Muslims enact during the annual pilgrimage to Mecca. All pilgrims must journey seven times between two locations identified as Ṣafā and Marwa that are located inside the enclosure of the Great Mosque in Mecca. In this way, they recall Hagar's frantic search for water for her son Ishmael/Ismāʿīl. Similarly, the well of Zamzam is a water source used by pilgrims inside the precincts of the mosque that is located near the Kaʿba.

Later exegetes strongly argued that it was Ishmael/Ismāʿīl, rather than Isaac/Isḥāq, who was Abraham's/Ibrāhīm's intended sacrifice, and they developed the idea of a counter covenant in which God granted special favor to the Arab Muslims through Ishmael/Ismāʿīl (Ibn Kathīr). Even though the son is not explicitly named in the Qur'anic text, later scholars contended that Ishmael/Ismā`īl was the "forbearing boy" whom Abraham/Ibrāhīm attempted to sacrifice. For instance, they note that there are two "glad tidings" of a boy in the sacrifice story—the first in 37:101, which begins the narrative, and the second in 37:112, which concludes it. They claim that the two glad tidings refer to two different sons, with the first being Ishmael/Ismā`īl and the second being Isaac/Isḥāq. In their view, the story of the near sacrifice found between the two describes what happens to the first of the two sons. In addition, they maintain that the Bible distorts the tradition by inserting Isaac's name into the text. In the biblical story (Gen. 22) God instructs Abraham/Ibrāhīm to sacrifice his "only son," which the Muslim exegetes argued could only be a reference to Ishmael/Ismā`īl since he was the older of the two sons. Because Ishmael/Ismā`īl was alive during Isaac's/Isḥāq's lifetime, the latter would not have been described as Abraham's/Ibrāhīm's only son. In addition, many prophetic traditions (*ḥadīth*) and statements from the companions of the Prophet Muhammad state that Ishmael/Ismā`īl, not Isaac/Isḥāq, was the intended sacrifice. Ishmael/Ismā`īl thus plays an important role in post-Qur'anic sources that explain how God created a new covenant with Arab Muslims.

Questions/Issues

(1) How does Ishmael's/Ismā`īl's association with the Ka`ba have an impact on his role and significance in Islam?
(2) How is the Islamic presentation of Ishmael/Ismā`īl similar to and different from that of his biblical counterpart?
(3) Which of Abraham's/Ibrāhīm's sons plays a more important role in Islam, Ishmael/Ismā`īl or Isaac/Isḥāq?
(4) What are your thoughts regarding how the Muslim tradition develops a counter Arab Muslim covenant with Ishmael/Ismā`īl being the son of Abraham/Ibrāhīm who was nearly sacrificed?

Further Reading

Firestone, Reuven. "Abraham's Son as the Intended Sacrifice (al-Dhabīh., Qur'ān 37:99–113): Issues in Qur'ānic Exegesis," *Journal of Semitic Studies* 34/1 (1989): 95–131.
Firestone, Reuven. *Journeys in Holy Lands. The Evolution of the Abraham-Ishmael Legends in Islamic Exegesis* (Albany, NY: State University of New York Press, 1990).

Firestone, Reuven. "Comparative Studies in Bible and Qur'ān: A Fresh Look at Genesis 22 in Light of Sura 37," in *Judaism and Islam: Boundaries, Communication and Interaction* ed. Benjamin H. Hary, John L. Hayes and Fred Astren (Leiden: Brill, 2000), pp. 169–84.

Mirza, Younus Y. "Ishmael as Abraham's Sacrifice: Ibn Taymiyya and Ibn Kathīr on the Intended Victim," *Islam and Christian—Muslim Relations* 24/3 (2013): 277–98.

Savant, Sarah Bowen. "Isaac as the Persians' Ishmael: Pride in the Pre-Islamic Past in Ninth and Tenth-century Islam," *Comparative Islamic Studies* 2/1 (2006): 5–25.

Wheeler, Brannon M. *Prophets in the Quran: An Introduction to the Quran and Muslim Exegesis* (London: Continuum, 2002), pp. 112–17.

22

Jacob/Ya`qūb

Qur'an 6:84; 19:49; 21:72; 38:45; 11:71; 29:27; 19:58; 12:1–102; 2:132–33

Jacob/Ya`qūb is a prophet, who is referred to sixteen times in the Qur'an. His name is most commonly found in various lists that include other important figures of the past. An example is seen in this instance, where Joseph/Yūsuf tells his fellow prisoners in Egypt, "I follow the religion of my fathers Abraham, Isaac, and Jacob" (12:38). Elsewhere in these lists Jacob/Ya`qūb is associated with particular qualities, including guidance from God (6:84), prophetic status (19:49), righteousness (21:72), and strength and vision (38:45; cf. 11:71; 29:27).

In two passages Jacob/Ya`qūb is identified as Israel/Isrā'īl, the other name by which he is known in the Bible. One of these texts states that the Israelites were allowed to eat any food "except that which Israel had forbidden for himself before the Torah was revealed" (3:93). The other instance is in a verse that concludes a discussion of several prophets by describing them as being of the "offspring of Abraham and Israel" (19:58). Jacob's/Ya`qūb's lineage is also mentioned in two texts that refer to the "House of Jacob/Ya`qūb" (12:6; 19:6). In the latter passage the phrase is found on the lips of Zachariah/Zakarīyyā, the father of John/Yaḥyā the Baptist.

The family of Jacob/Ya`qūb figures prominently in chapter 12, the longest single narrative in the Qur'an, which recounts how his son Joseph/Yūsuf is betrayed by his brothers and sent to Egypt. The account opens with Jacob/Ya`qūb warning Joseph/Yūsuf not to tell his brothers about a dream he has had, and informing him that God will choose him and teach him how to interpret dreams and events (12:6). After the brothers sell Joseph/Yūsuf to Egypt they return home to their father, who sees through their attempt to trick him into thinking that Joseph/Yūsuf has been killed by an animal. "No! Rather, your minds have led you to make up this story. Beautiful patience! God is the one whose help is sought against what you have described" (12:19). Later in the story, when the brothers go to Egypt in search of food because there is a famine in their land, Joseph/Yūsuf sends them back so they might return to him with the brother they left at home. Jacob/Ya`qūb is initially hesitant to agree to this plan, but he ultimately acquiesces. The text indicates that Jacob/Ya`qūb was able to do this because he had been specially favored by God. "Truly, he possessed knowledge that We taught him, but most people do not know" (12:68). The special knowledge that God gave to him is mentioned by Jacob/Ya`qūb himself in a later scene when he expresses his continuing grief over the loss of Joseph/Yūsuf. "I complain of my sorrow and sadness to God. I know from God that which you do not know" (12:86). The brothers return to Joseph/Yūsuf again and he reveals his true identity to them, at which point he sends them back home with his shirt to help heal their father's blindness. When his eyesight returns, Jacob/Ya`qūb makes a further reference to the knowledge that God has granted him (12:93–98). The story concludes with Jacob/Ya`qūb returning with his other sons to Egypt to be reunited with Joseph/Yūsuf, who honors his parents by bringing them close to his throne.

Jacob's/Ya`qūb's final words are recorded in this verse, when he tells his sons, "God has chosen the proper religion for you, so do not die without submitting" (2:132–33). With his dying words Jacob/Ya`qūb asks his sons what they will serve after he is gone, and they respond by saying that they will serve and submit themselves to the God that he and his ancestors worshipped.

Questions/Issues

(1) What are the main features of the way that Jacob/Ya`qūb is portrayed in the Muslim sources?

(2) Compare the character of Jacob/Ya`qūb in the Joseph/Yūsuf story in chapter 12 in the Qur'an with his counterpart in Genesis 37–50.

(3) Why is the theme of the knowledge he has received from God an important part of the Qur'an's presentation of Jacob/Ya`qūb?

Further Reading

Wheeler, Brannon M. *Prophets in the Quran: An Introduction to the Quran and Muslim Exegesis* (London: Continuum, 2002), pp. 112–17.

23

Jesus/`Īsā

Qur'an 3:42–47; 19:16–29; 4:171; 5:46; 3:45; 66:12; 2:87, 253; 5:110; 5:17, 72–76, 116–17; 19:30–31; 3:49; 43:57, 59; 4:157–58; 61:6

The prophet and messenger Jesus/`Īsā is mentioned by name twenty-five times in the Qur'an. On nine occasions the name appears by itself, and the other sixteen times it is found in combination with the descriptors "son of Mary" and/or "Messiah." The phrase "son of Mary" is found twenty-three times in the Qur'an, twice by itself and elsewhere with "Jesus/`Īsā," "the Messiah," or "the Messiah Jesus/`Īsā." In contrast, it appears only once in the New Testament in the question, "Is this not the carpenter, the son of Mary?" (Mk 6:3). The frequent use of "son of Mary" in the Qur'an is likely a way of underscoring the humanity of Jesus/`Īsā, which is a central theme in many of the passages that refer to him.

There is no single cohesive narrative in the Qur'an that describes the events of Jesus's/`Īsā's life similar to what is contained in the four Gospels of the New Testament. In fact, there is very little overlap with the scenes and episodes described in the Christian writings because the Qur'an is typically more concerned with clarifying who Jesus/`Īsā was than with explaining what he did. An exception to this are two passages that describe how Jesus/`Īsā was conceived, one of which also provides an account of his birth (3:42–47; 19:16–29). Both of these texts, like the Gospels of Matthew and Luke, maintain that Jesus/`Īsā was virginally conceived, because his mother Mary/Maryam did not become pregnant through sexual relations with a man.

The Qur'an's Christology, or view of Jesus/`Īsā, is summed up neatly in this verse, which reads in part, "Truly, the Messiah Jesus, son of Mary, was God's messenger, His word He sent to Mary, and a spirit from Him" (4:171). Three different roles that Jesus/`Īsā played, in addition to that of Messiah, are identified in this passage. He was one of God's messengers, and elsewhere the Qur'an explains that he delivered the message in the form of a written book known as the *injīl*. This term is probably an Arabized form of *euangelion*, the Greek word for "gospel." The relationship between this message and prior revelation is explained in this verse. "We sent after them (the prophets) Jesus, son of Mary, attesting to the truth already in the Torah. We gave him the *injīl* containing guidance and light, attesting to the truth already in the Torah. It is a guidance and exhortation for the faithful ones" (5:46). This verse explains how Jesus/ʿĪsā is in the line of the earlier prophets, and that he delivered a message to his people that confirmed the legitimacy of the previous revelation.

The passage goes on to say that he was God's word, a term also used in reference to Jesus/ʿĪsā in 3:45. Jesus/ʿĪsā is similarly described in the New Testament at the beginning of the Gospel according to John, where he is presented as God's word that became human (Jn 1:1–18). Although the terminology is the same, the Qur'an's reference to Jesus/ʿĪsā as God's word is different from that of the New Testament, where it is a way of speaking about Jesus's/ʿĪsā's equality with God. Such a view would be inconsistent with Islam's understanding of the deity, and so the notion of Jesus/ʿĪsā as God's word in the Qur'an refers to the divine message he brought to his people as a prophet. It might also be an allusion to the word from God that Mary/Maryam received from the angel when she was told that she was pregnant. The third way that Jesus/ʿĪsā is spoken of in 4:171 is as God's spirit, another term that conveys a different sense than what it does for Christians when they read it in the New Testament. Here, too, it should be interpreted in connection with the Qur'an's description of Jesus's/ʿĪsā's conception. In 66:12 God breathes His spirit into Mary/Maryam in order to impregnate her, and in this way Jesus/ʿĪsā is a spirit from God. A number of other passages explain how God strengthens and comforts Jesus/ʿĪsā with His spirit, and perhaps these texts also help to explain the close connection between God's spirit and Jesus/ʿĪsā (2:87, 253; 5:110).

In addition to its statements regarding who Jesus/ʿĪsā was, this verse also provides information about who he was not, according to the Qur'an. "So believe in God and His messengers, and do not say, 'Three.' Desist and it will be better for you because, truly, God is one God. It is beyond Him to have a son. All that is in the heavens and on the earth belongs to Him. God is the only protector" (4:171). Coming immediately after the section of the verse quoted earlier, this portion of it is a clear condemnation of Christian beliefs about Jesus/ʿĪsā, even though he is not cited by name. Specifically, it repudiates two basic tenets of Christian theology—the Trinity, or belief that God is three persons in one ("Do not say, 'Three.'"), and the incarnation, which holds that Jesus/ʿĪsā was God in human form ("It is beyond Him to have a son."). Both of these beliefs are examples of the sin of *shirk*, associating something from creation with the uncreated deity in a way that compromises the divine unity, and the Qur'an rejects them in a number of passages. This rejection is succinctly stated in this verse. "They have disbelieved who say, 'Truly, God is the Messiah, the son of Mary'" (5:17; cf. 5:72–76).

A bit later in the same chapter is found a passage that is difficult for Christians to accept for two reasons—it presents an understanding of the Trinity that is at odds with orthodox Christian belief, and it has Jesus/ʿĪsā himself deny the Trinity and the incarnation.

> God said, "Oh Jesus, son of Mary, did you ever say to people, 'Take me and my mother as two gods apart from God?'" He said, "Praise be to You! It is not for me to say that of which I have no right. If I had said it, You surely would have known it. You know what is in my mind, but I do not know what is in Your mind. You are the knower of hidden things. I did not say anything to them except that which You commanded me to say—'Worship God, my Lord and your Lord.' I was a witness over them for as long as I was among them. And when You took me to Yourself, You were the one who watched over them. You are a witness over all things." (5:116–17)

This passage appears to claim that Christians worship Mary/Maryam as a deity and that they consider her to be a part of the Trinity. Such a belief does not reflect mainstream Christian theology, although throughout history some Christian groups have so highly venerated Mary/Maryam that it might appear to an outsider that she has been given divine status. Such an interpretation of Christian belief and practice might underlie what is stated in this Qur'an passage. While Jesus/ʿĪsā repudiates the notion that he is divine, it is important to keep in mind that this is due to Islamic teaching about God's unity, and does not reflect hatred or animosity toward Christianity. According to the Qur'an, notions like Trinity and incarnation are at odds with the belief in God's oneness and are therefore to be avoided. This is why Jesus/ʿĪsā places himself in a position of inferiority to God in this passage as he stresses the deity's omniscience and his own complete obedience to the divine will ("I did not say anything to them except that which You commanded me to say.").

The same deferential attitude toward God on Jesus's/ʿĪsā's part can be seen in another passage that recounts his words as a newborn, when his mother returned with him to her people. "I am the servant of God. He has given me the book, and has made me a prophet. He has made me blessed wherever I may be, and He has commanded me to observe prayer and give alms for as long as I live" (19:30–31). Despite his tender age as an infant, Jesus/ʿĪsā makes it clear that he is well aware of the nature of the relationship that exists between himself and God. His very first words leave no doubt about the matter—"I am the servant of God." Throughout the Qur'an Jesus/ʿĪsā is quick to point out that he is a human being like anyone else, and that God is "my Lord and your Lord." That point is reiterated several times in the verses as he explains that his role as a messenger and prophet is not something he has accomplished on his own, but rather has been bestowed on him by God. The command for him to observe prayer and almsgiving is interesting because these are two of the five pillars of Islam. Here, as with other biblical figures elsewhere in the Qur'an, Jesus/ʿĪsā is presented as a true believer who has submitted himself fully to the divine will and whose faith coheres with the message that Muhammad will deliver centuries later.

The Qur'an teaches that Jesus's/ʿĪsā's first miracle was his ability to speak as an infant, and other passages refer to the works of wonder he will perform as an adult. Here, too, he consistently points beyond himself to God as the one who is behind all that he does. "I have come to you with a sign from your Lord. I will make a bird-shaped form out of clay for you and then breathe into it and, with God's permission, it will become a real bird. I will heal the blind and the leprous, and I will bring the dead back to life, with God's permission" (3:49). As in the New Testament, the Jesus/ʿĪsā of the Qur'an is able to perform miracles like healing the sick and raising the dead, but with the double mention of "with God's permission" he reminds people that the deity is ultimately the one behind these magnificent feats and he is nothing more than God's instrument. The reference to the clay bird that is brought to life is intriguing in light of the fact that he performs a similar miracle in a Christian writing known as "The Infancy Gospel of Thomas" that can be traced back to the second century CE. The mention of it here raises interesting questions about how familiar Muhammad and the early Muslim community might have been with Christians and their written sources in the formative years of Islam.

Some of the key themes of Jesus's/ʿĪsā's teachings in the New Testament are not mentioned in the Qur'an, including the kingdom of God/kingdom of heaven, social justice, forgiveness, the end times, and concern for the poor and marginalized in society. The same is true with the form that his teaching takes. He speaks in parables often in the synoptic gospels, but he does not use this manner of communicating in the Qur'an. Although he does not speak in parables in the Qur'an, in a couple of places Jesus/ʿĪsā is described as a *mathal*, which is the Arabic term for a parable that is often translated as "example" in these verses (43:57, 59).

Jesus/ʿĪsā appears to allude to his own death in the verse cited earlier when he says to God, "when You took me to Yourself" (5:117). His death is referred to in a few places in the Qur'an, but there is no description of it and it does not play a salvific role for humanity as it does in the New Testament. The Qur'an's most important passage related to Jesus's/ʿĪsā's death is this one:

> They said, "We killed the Messiah Jesus, son of Mary, God's messenger." They did not kill him nor did they crucify him, but it was made to appear so to them. They who disagree about it are truly in grave doubt over it. They have no knowledge about it, and only follow conjecture. Surely, they did not kill him. Rather, God raised him to Himself. God is the mighty one, the wise one. (4:157–58)

The larger literary context of this passage indicates that the ones referred to as "they" are the Jews who were Jesus's/ʿĪsā's contemporaries. The section prior to these verses identifies a number of ways in which the Jews went against God's will throughout history, and this passage says that they continued that pattern when they claimed responsibility for Jesus's/ʿĪsā's death. They were mistaken in this thinking, however, because God was in control the entire time, and allowed Jesus/ʿĪsā to die before taking him to Himself, as is also stated in 3:54–55. It seemed to the Jews that they were in charge of things, but the death of Jesus/ʿĪsā was part of the divine plan.

An interesting aspect of 4:157–58 is that its meaning is ambiguous, because one section of it can be read in two ways. The key phrase in Arabic is *shubbiḥa laḥum*, which is translated here as "it was made to appear so to them." Another way it can be rendered is "he was made to appear so to them," in which case the focus is on Jesus/ʿĪsā himself rather than the circumstances of his death. If the latter translation is adopted, then it is possible to read the verse as claiming that it was not actually Jesus/ʿĪsā who died. This alternative reading has given rise to the view that is fairly common among Qur'an commentators and other Muslims that someone else was substituted for Jesus/ʿĪsā and took his place on the cross. The grammatical ambiguity is completely unresolvable, so either interpretation is possible.

A final Qur'an passage mentioning Jesus/ʿĪsā that should be considered is this one, where he apparently predicts the coming of Muhammad. "I am God's messenger to you, attesting to the truth already in the Torah and announcing the good news of a messenger who will come after me whose name is Ahmad" (61:6). The three root letters of the Arabic word "Ahmad" are the same as those in "Muhammad," and the two names are considered to be variants of each other. The Qur'an therefore quotes Jesus/ʿĪsā foretelling the coming of the prophet of Islam more than five centuries before his birth. It should be noted that it is common for Muslims to claim that Jesus/ʿĪsā makes the same prediction in the New Testament when, in the Gospel according to John, he asks God to send an advocate or helper to assist his community in his absence (Jn 14:16; 15:26). The identification of this advocate figure with Muhammad is helped by the fact that in the Syriac translation of the New Testament, the form of the text with which early Muslims would have been most familiar, the word for "advocate" sounds very much like "Muhammad."

"The Stories of the Prophets" literature uses the story of Jesus/ʿĪsā to emphasize monotheism. God could not have a son because he created everything and is the master over all things. Every creature needs him and is dependent on his divine being. Everything in the heavens and on the earth are his servants. He is the Lord, there is no god except him. The commentators stress that monotheism is a consistent theme in the Qur'an and that no creature could share God's unique nature. For instance, the Qur'an condemns pagan Arabs for holding the polytheist belief that God had angels as daughters (43:19; 37:26–29) and certain Jews for believing that Ezra/ʿUzayr was the son of God (9:30). The Qur'an's critiques of Christianity are thus consistent with its critiques of other religious communities who believed that certain figures shared God's unique nature. In particular, the literature speaks to how Muslims understand Jesus/ʿĪsā in relation to Jews and Christians. Some Jews say that he was a child of adultery, while the Christians say that he is God or the child of God. In contrast, Muslims say that he was the servant of God and his messenger (Ibn Kathīr).

The literature also emphasizes the many miracles of Jesus/ʿĪsā. In addition to his miraculous birth and his ability to speak in his cradle, Jesus/ʿĪsā performed various miracles as a child. One popular story relates that when Jesus/ʿĪsā would play with other children he would ask them, "Do you want me to tell you what your mother has saved for you [to eat]?" They would say yes, and he would inform them. They would then run back to their mothers and ask them to give them what they were saving for them. The mothers would ask, "What thing did I save for you?" and the children would respond by naming the exact thing. Surprised, the mothers would inquire, "Who informed you of this?" The children would say, "Jesus/ʿĪsā, the son of Mary/Maryam" (Ibn Kathīr).

In another story, a young Jesus/ʿĪsā was playing with some children when an older boy came and kicked one of the children and killed him. The boy then threw the body of the child in front of Jesus/ʿĪsā. When the people heard the news of the boy's death, they came to the scene and saw Jesus/ʿĪsā next to the body and subsequently blamed him for the child's death. They then took Jesus/ʿĪsā to the judge, who asked him if he killed the boy. Jesus/ʿĪsā said that he did not know who killed the boy and that he was the child's friend. The group wanted to seize Jesus/`Īsā but before they could do so he said, "Bring the child to me." They asked, "What do you want with him?" and he calmly responded, "I want to ask him who killed him." They inquired bewilderedly, "How can he speak to you when he is dead?" Nevertheless, they took Jesus/`Īsā to the dead boy. Jesus/`Īsā then started to pray, and God brought the boy back to life. He then asked the boy who killed him, and he identified the guilty party. Jesus/`Īsā then returned to his mother with a large group of people and his mother said to him, "Oh son, did I not prevent you from doing this?" to which Jesus/`Īsā responded, "Verily, God will protect us, he is the most merciful." As he got older, Jesus/`Īsā continued to perform miracles because God gave him the ability to walk on water, heal lepers, and cure the blind. The various miracle stories all highlight how Jesus/`Īsā was special even at a young age, and how he performed miracles with God's permission (al-Thaʿlabī).

Other traditions highlight Jesus's/`Īsā's asceticism. He would wear wool, eat leaves, and not live in a house. He had no money or family, and he would not save anything for the following day. One tradition states that, "Verily Jesus/`Īsā will be the head of the ascetics on the Day of Resurrection," while another states that, "those fleeing from their sins will gather around Jesus/`Īsā on the Day of Resurrection." The traditions explain that Jesus/`Īsā was constantly thinking about the hereafter, and they claim that those seeking repentance will seek him out.

"The Stories of the Prophets" literature also captures some of Jesus's/`Īsā's aphorisms in which he speaks about worldly detachment. In one saying he states, "Oh weak child of Adam, be conscious of God wherever you are, be in this world as a guest, take the mosque as your house, teach your eyes to cry, your body to be patient and your heart to contemplate. Do not concern yourself with tomorrow's sustenance; verily that would be a mistake." Another speaks of avoiding falling in love with this world. "The love of this world is the beginning of every mistake, and looking [at what is not permissible] plants desire in the heart." An additional one states, "Love of this world and love of the hereafter do not settle in the heart of a believer, just as water and fire do not settle in a container." A similar message is conveyed in one in which he says, "the seeker of this world is similar to the drinker of the water of the ocean; the more they drink, the more they become thirsty until they die."

The Qur'an verse (61:6) in which Jesus/`Īsā speaks about the coming of Muhammad is also mentioned in "The Stories of the Prophets." The tradition states that God told Jesus/`Īsā that Muhammad would eventually come after him, and that he would guide people who are going astray, teach them, bring them out of ignorance, and enrich them after they become impoverished. Jesus/ʿĪsā is also told that Muhammad's community will be the best community, and they will establish the good and forbid the evil (Ibn Kathīr).

The literature largely endorses the "substitution theory" that Jesus/ʿĪsā himself did not die on the cross, but rather someone was made to look like him. In one popular story, the guards encircled Jesus's/ʿĪsā's house while he was inside with his disciples, and when they entered God made all the disciples look like Jesus/ʿĪsā. The guards then said, "You have bewitched us! Bring out Jesus/ʿĪsā, or we will kill all of you!" Then Jesus/ʿĪsā asked his companions, "Which of you today would like to go to paradise?" One of the companions said that he wished to do so, and the man went to the guards and said, "I am Jesus/ʿĪsā." The tradition reports that the guards then crucified him, thinking that they killed Jesus/ʿĪsā. Another popular story explains how God made Judas, the betrayer of Jesus/ʿĪsā, look like Jesus/ʿĪsā and was then killed and crucified in his place (Ibn Kathīr).

Questions/Issues

(1) When considering how Jesus/ʿĪsā is presented in the Islamic sources and the Bible, are the similarities or the differences more striking for you?
(2) Which of the two possibilities for reading the ambiguous passage in the Qur'an about the death of Jesus/ʿĪsā seems more plausible?
(3) What is your reaction to Jesus's/ʿĪsā's prediction of the coming of Muhammad in the Qur'an and other Muslim sources?

Further Reading

Ayoub, Mahmoud M. "Towards an Islamic Christology, II: The Death of Jesus, Reality or Delusion," *The Muslim World* 70/2 (1980): 91–121.
Parrinder, Geoffrey. *Jesus in the Qur'an*; reprint (Oxford: Oneworld Publications, 2013).
Robinson, Neal. *Christ in Islam and Christianity: Representation of Jesus in the Qur'an and the Classical Muslim Commentaries* (New York: Palgrave Macmillan, 1991).

24

Jews

Qur'an 5:18; 2:13, 120; 6:146; 9:30; 5:64, 70; 2:61, 87, 91; 3:21, 112, 181, 183; 4:155; 2:75; 4:46; 5:13, 41–43; 6:91; 2:62; 5:69; 6:146; 4:160; 5:41; 16:118; 62:6; 7:104–5, 134, 137–38; 10:90, 93; 20:47, 80; 26:17, 22; 44:30–32; 2:40, 47, 83, 122; 5:12; 17:2; 32:23; 40:53; 45:16; 3:43; 5:72, 110; 43:59; 61:6, 14; 2:122; 4:162; 7:159

Judaism was well established in Arabia during the formative period of Islam, and the religion's roots in that part of the world can be traced to at least the first century CE. A number of Jewish tribes are mentioned by name in the Islamic sources, which indicates that Muhammad and the early Muslims had more contact with Jews than they had with Christians. This was especially true after the *Hijrah* of 622 CE, when Muhammad and a small group of his followers migrated from Mecca to Medina. There was a sizable Jewish community in the latter city, where Muhammad had been invited to serve as an arbiter who was asked to resolve conflicts among Jews and other members of Medinan society. Islamic sources, such as the biography of Muhammad's life, explain that the relationship between him and the Jews of Medina was sometimes contentious. These works report that the local Jewish tribes occasionally assisted Muhammad's enemies in Mecca and elsewhere in their attacks against the Muslims, and, in order to help his nascent community survive, he retaliated in turn. Several graphic episodes are recorded in these writings that describe the mass execution of Jewish men and the enslavement of Jewish women and children. As will be explained below, this context should be kept in mind when considering what the Qur'an and other Islamic sources have to say about Jews and how Muslims should relate to them.

The Arabic term the Qur'an uses for Jews, which probably comes from Hebrew, is *yahūd* (singular, *yahūdī*). It is found nine times in the text, six of which also mention Christians, and all of these passages express negative views toward Jews. In the following verse Jewish (and Christian) claims that they are God's favorites are challenged as misguided.

> The Jews and the Christians say, "We are the children of God and His beloved ones." Say (Muhammad), "Then why does He punish you for your offenses? You are merely among the people He has created. He forgives whomever He will, and punishes whomever He will. God has authority over the heavens and the earth and all that is between them. Everything leads to Him." (5:18)

In other places the Qur'an identifies a number of the offenses that this passage says the Jews are guilty of, including accusing each other of wrongdoing (2:113), not accepting Muhammad as God's prophet (2:120), disobedience (6:146), and claiming someone named Ezra/`Uzayr was God's son (9:30). Perhaps the Qur'an's harshest verse against the Jews can be found at 5:64, which criticizes them for not recognizing God's power, not accepting the Qur'an as God's word, waging war, and spreading corruption.

A theologically serious transgression that the Qur'an charges Jews with is their inability to accept either God's prophets or their messages. In multiple passages it is stated that emissaries commissioned by the deity have been mistreated by Jews, who refused to believe them. "We made a covenant with the children of Israel, and We sent messengers to them. Every time a messenger brought something they did not like, they accused some of them of lying and they put others to death" (5:70; cf. 2:61, 87, 91; 3:21, 112, 181, 183; 4:155). Related to this is the accusation that the Jews tampered with and falsified the divine revelation that had been delivered by the prophets, an offense identified in Arabic as *taḥrīf*. "How can you hope that they will believe you, when a group of them used to hear the word of God and then distorted it after they had understood it?" (2:75; cf. 4:46; 5:13, 41–43; 6:91). The same charge is leveled against Christians, and it is a way in which the text tries to explain why there are differences between the Bible and the Qur'an. Islam teaches that God delivered the same message to all of the prophets throughout history, and it was the message of submission to the divine will (*islām* in Arabic). The followers of the earlier prophets did not accurately pass on the content of that message, and this necessitated the sending of the final prophet Muhammad with the perfectly preserved message of the Qur'an.

Another way the Qur'an refers to Jews is by using an Arabic verb (*hāda*) that means "to be or become a Jew." It appears approximately twelve times in the text, and it is sometimes employed to speak of Jews in a positive way. For example, it is found in a verse that describes the rewards that will come to members of a number of religious groups. "Regarding believers, Jews, Christians, and

Sabians—those who believe in God and the last day, and do good deeds—their reward is with their Lord. No fear will come upon them, nor will they grieve" (2:62; cf. 5:69). Elsewhere the same Arab verb is found in verses that adopt the more critical view of Jews that is typical of the Qur'an. This can be seen in a verse that presents the Jewish dietary restrictions as a punishment that is due to their lack of belief. "For the Jews We prohibited animals with claws, and the fat of cattle and sheep, except what is on their backs, in their entrails, or attached to their bones. That is how We paid them back for their disobedience. Indeed, We are truthful" (6:146; cf. 4:46, 160; 5:41; 16:118; 62:6).

As seen above in 5:70, a term related to the Jewish community that is frequently used in the Qur'an is "the Children of Israel" (*bānū isrā'īl* in Arabic). It appears approximately forty times in the text, but never in reference to Jews living during Muhammad's lifetime. It rather always refers to the Israelites of biblical times, and more than one-half of the occurrences of the phrase "the Children of Israel" describe people who were contemporaries of Moses/Mūsā, especially those who escaped with him from Egypt and Pharaoh/Fir`awn during the Exodus (7:104–5, 134, 137–38; 10:90, 93; 20:47, 80; 26:17, 22; 44:30). Other themes addressed in passages that mention the Children of Israel include the covenantal promise God made with them (2:40, 47, 83, 122; 5:12; 20:80), and the Torah as the revealed book that God gave to Moses/Mūsā for them (17:2; 32:23; 40:53; 45:16). In six passages, the Children of Israel are mentioned in relation to Jesus/`Īsā, and in two of them he addresses them using that title (3:43; 5:72, 110; 43:59; 61:6, 14).

A number of Qur'an texts mention God's choice of Israel and the special relationship that the Jews had with God. "Oh Children of Israel, remember how I favored you and privileged you over other people" (2:47; cf. 2:122; 44:30–32). The Arabic term for that bond is *mīthāq*, which also describes other types of relationships in the Qur'an. When it is used in reference to the one between Israel and God, it is often translated as "covenant." As already noted, the Qur'an agrees with the biblical tradition in its claim that the Israelites sometimes fell short and did not live up to the terms of their relationship with God. "But they violated their covenant (*mīthāq*), so We rejected them and hardened their hearts" (5:13a). This is what allowed for the transfer of the covenant from the Israelites to the Muslims, and the apologetic nature of this theme is important to keep in mind. The Qur'an's presentation of the Israelites as unreliable covenant partners with God mirrors the difficult relationship Muhammad had with his Jewish contemporaries, whose perceived disloyalty to him is what caused the split between them. Their ancestors' earlier inability to stay faithful in their relationship with God establishes the paradigm and legitimates Muhammad's actions against the Jews of his own day.

Several Qur'an passages adopt a more positive and conciliatory tone toward Jews and Judaism, as seen in 2:62 which was cited above. At times, a distinction is made between Jews who are good and those who are not. One verse concludes a list of Jewish offenses by stating that those who do not take part in these activities will not be punished. "Those among them who are steeped in knowledge and are faithful, they believe in what has been revealed to you (Muhammad) and what has been revealed before you. Those who engage in prayer, pay alms, and believe in God and the last day—to them We will give a great reward" (4:162; cf. 4:46; 7:159). The reference in this verse to what was revealed to Muhammad could mean that only those Jews who become Muslims will be rewarded, and if it is interpreted in that way then the passage is less positive about Jews than it appears to be. On the other hand, those things identified as exemplary—prayer, almsgiving, and belief in God and the last day—are all central to Judaism, and so the passage could be saying that Jews need only follow the dictates of their religion to avoid punishment.

This overview indicates that most of the references to Jews and Judaism in the Qur'an evaluate them negatively. At the same time, it is important to note that the vast majority of the passages discussed and listed here that are most critical are found in chapters that come from the time that Muhammad was in Medina. As noted earlier, relations between Muslims and Jews were often quite tense during that period, and it is likely that much of the negativity toward Judaism present in these texts is due to and reflects the problems that existed between the two groups at that point in time. In other words, these passages are primarily responding to a particular context and set of circumstances in Arabia of the seventh century CE, in which the early Muslim community was experiencing hostility and resistance from members of the Jewish community in Medina. Consequently, commentators have sometimes argued that these texts are relevant only for their own time and place, and they should not be used as a guide for how later Muslims should view Judaism and relate to Jews.

A final point to consider is that, as with Christianity and its followers, it is not always entirely clear who or what the Qur'an is referring to when it mentions Jews and Judaism. In particular, it could be that Muhammad and the early Muslims came in contact with Jews whose beliefs and practices did not perfectly align with what has come to be viewed as mainstream Judaism. This can be seen in an enigmatic verse mentioned above that claims that the Jews take a man named Ezra to be the son of God (9:30). There is no evidence for such a belief within Jewish sources, and for a discussion of this passage please see the entry titled "Ezra/ʿUzayr" in this book.

Questions/Issues

(1) How important is it to keep their original contexts in mind when considering what the Qur'an and other Islamic sources have to say about Jews and Judaism?
(2) Should these sources be used to inform modern-day views about how Muslims and Jews should interact?
(3) What are some of the main reasons why tensions sometimes exist between religious communities?

Further Reading

Sachedina, Abdulaziz A. "Jews, Christians, and Muslims according to the Qur'an," *Greek Orthodox Theological Review* 31/1 (1986), 105–20.

25

Jinn

Qur'an 18:50; 51:56–58; 32:13; 6:128; 7:38, 179; 11:119; 37:158; 55:39; 72:1–15; 46:29–31; 15:16–18; 37:6–10; 27:17, 39; 34:12; 21:82; 38:37; 34:14; 55:33

The jinn (singular *jinnī*) are nonhuman created beings who are mentioned approximately thirty times in the Qur'an. Belief in the jinn (from which the English word "genie" comes) among the Arabs predated Islam. They were invisible creatures, often associated with parts of the natural world, who interacted with humans in both positive and negative ways. The phrase "jinn and humans" (or vice versa) is found twenty times in the Qur'an, indicating the close connection between their two spheres of existence. The only one of the jinn named in the text is Iblīs, who refused God's command to kneel before Adam/ Ādam. He is identified as a *jinnī* in 18:50, but elsewhere he is described as a disobedient angel.

Like human beings, the jinn's main purpose is to acknowledge and honor God. "I created jinn and humanity only to worship Me. I do not want them to provide for Me or to feed Me. God is the One who provides, the Lord of power, the strong One" (51:56–58). In this text and elsewhere, the Qur'an places the jinn in a subordinate position to God and thereby limits the power and abilities they had in the pre-Islamic period. At the same time, they are capable of leading people to ruin, and will themselves experience eternal punishment as a result. "If We had wished, We would have given every soul its proper guidance. But My words are true—I will surely fill hell with jinn and people together" (32:13; cf. 6:128; 7:38, 179; 11:119; 37:158; 55:39; 72:5–6).

The jinn can also guide people in the proper way and remind them to follow God's will. The first fifteen verses of chapter 72 in the Qur'an, which bears the title "The Jinn," urge Muhammad to tell his people about a group of jinn who hear the Qur'an and immediately express their belief in it. They profess their faith in some of the basic tenets of Islam, while acknowledging that not all of their fellow jinn have been as receptive to the Qur'an's message and will suffer in hell for their lack of belief. This text serves as a warning to Muhammad's audience to not follow the way of the unbelieving jinn. The same message is conveyed in the following verse:

> We sent a group of jinn to you (Muhammad) to listen to the Qur'an. When they were there they said to one another, "Be quiet!" When it was over, they warned their fellow jinn and said, "Oh our people, we have been listening to a revelation sent down after Moses that validates what came before it and gives guidance to the truth and the straight path. Oh our people, respond to the one who summons you to God's name and believe in Him! He will forgive your sins and will protect you from a painful punishment." (46:29–31)

Some commentators have associated the jinn with the satans (*shayāṭīn*), another group sometimes mentioned in the Qur'an (15:16–18; 37:6–10; 72:8–9). This association is supported by certain traditions about Solomon/Sulaymān, the biblical figure whose story contains the most references to jinn in the Qur'an. In some passages it is stated that the jinn served King Solomon/Sulaymān (27:17, 39; 34:12), but elsewhere it is the satans who do his bidding (21:82; 38:37). One tradition states that the jinn did not realize that Solomon/Sulaymān had died until a small animal gnawed at the staff he was leaning on and caused his corpse to fall to the ground, a further indication of their limitations and lack of full knowledge in the Qur'an (34:14).

The Qur'an describes the jinn in a way consistent with how it views the rest of the created order. They are creatures who are totally dependent on God for their existence, and they must submit themselves to the divine will in a way that makes them a sign of God's supreme power. "O company of jinn and humanity, if you are able to pass through all the regions of heaven and earth, then pass through. But you cannot pass through without (Our) authority" (55:33).

Questions/Issues

(1) Do Judaism or Christianity have any creatures who are like the jinn?
(2) What does the role of the jinn in the Qur'an suggest about the text's view of humanity?
(3) How do the jinn contribute to the Islamic view of God?

Further Reading

El-Zein, Amira. *Islam, Arabs, and the Intelligent World of the Jinn* (Syracuse: Syracuse University Press, 2009).

26

Job/Ayyūb

Qur'an 4:163–65; 6:83–90; 21:83–84; 38:41–44

Job/Ayyūb is a prophet who is mentioned four times in the Qur'an. In 6:83–90 he is listed as one of eighteen individuals who, because of their good works, have been chosen by God to receive guidance and favor in the form of scripture, wisdom, and status as a prophet. All eighteen of these people are biblical figures, and the text urges that they and their teachings should be followed. Two chapters earlier Job/Ayyūb and most of the others listed are described as having received divine revelation (4:163–65).

The other two passages relate more directly to Job's/Ayyūb's character in the Bible by identifying qualities that set him apart from others. He is presented as an example to be remembered in 21:83–84, where he cries out that his suffering might be taken away. God hears his cry, removes his affliction, and returns his family to him, including some new members. The text lacks a narrative that describes these events in detail, but the pattern of human appeal, divine response, and restoration mirrors what takes place in the biblical story where Job/Ayyūb cries out to God after losing everything, God responds, and Job's/Ayyūb's possessions are returned to him. The Qur'an passage concludes with a statement that these things happened to Job/Ayyūb so they can serve as a reminder for all God's servants.

The description of Job/Ayyūb in 38:41–44 is more narrative-like. It begins with him crying out for assistance as 21:83–84 does, but this time he identifies Satan/Shayṭān as the cause of his weariness and pain. He then is told (presumably by God) to stomp his foot, which leads to the appearance of a pool of water that enables him to bathe and drink. This is followed by a reference to his family being restored to him, again in a number greater than they originally were, and a reminder that Job's/Ayyūb's recovery is a sign to all of the presence and possibility of divine mercy. He is then instructed to take some twigs in his hand and to strike someone (or something) in order to fulfill an oath he has made. The passage concludes with a description of Job/Ayyūb as a patient person, who always turned to God.

Similar to the biblical tradition, in this passage Satan/Shayṭān is identified as the cause of Job's/Ayyūb's problems, and the mention of his repentance is in line with his character as it is presented in the Bible. The two commands that Job/Ayyūb stomp on the ground and take some twigs to hit something or someone with them are not in the Bible. A number of gaps exist in the Qur'an text. For example, the details about the unexpected water source that appears when Job/Ayyūb stomps his foot are not explained. Similarly, nothing is said about what or whom Job/Ayyūb should strike with the twigs, or the content of the oath he has sworn.

The image of Job/Ayyūb that is found in the Qur'an is consistent and clear—he is an individual who remains faithful and steadfast in the midst of his troubles, and as such is a reminder and an example for others.

"The Stories of the Prophets" and exegetical literature expand upon the concise Qur'anic narrative. The literature notes that Job/Ayyūb had a tremendous amount of wealth, ranging from cattle to agriculture. However, when he became sick he lost all of his money and his body became weak, except for his heart and tongue which he would remember God by. Everyone deserted Job/Ayyūb except for his caring and patient wife, who continued to serve him and tend to his needs. Some commentators, like al-Thaʿlabī, note that his wife's name was Raḥma or "mercy." The situation became so dire that she started to work as a servant so she could earn money to feed Job/Ayyūb and take care of him. However, people did not want to employ her because they knew that she was the wife of Job/Ayyūb and they feared contracting his sickness. Since no one would hire her, she resorted to selling one of her braids to a group of noble women for a large amount of food. When she brought the food to Job/Ayyūb he became shocked and asked, "Where did you get this food?" to which she replied that she worked as a servant. However, the next day she still could not find someone who would hire her, so she sold her other braid. This time Job/Ayyūb swore that he would not eat it until she told him how she got the food. She then removed her scarf from her head, which was completely shaved. When Job/Ayyūb saw her shaven head he then began his prayer, "Suffering has truly afflicted me, but you are the most merciful of the merciful." God then ordered Job/Ayyūb to stomp on the ground from which two springs emerged, one of which he drank from while the other he bathed in. Once he bathed in the spring, all of his pain and aliments vanished, and he was reunited with his family and friends.

Qur'anic commentators also fill in the details of whom Job/Ayyūb was supposed to hit and for what reason. A dominant interpretation states that one day, in a state of frustration and anger, Job/Ayyūb swore to strike his wife one hundred times. Different reasons are given for this oath, ranging from her lack of care to her selling one of her braids in order to feed him. After Job/Ayyūb became well, God ordered him to reduce the severity of the oath by gathering a hundred twigs and then hitting her only once. Thus, the Stories of the Prophet literature emphasizes the remarkable patience of Job/Ayyūb and his wife, which is eventually rewarded by God through the return of his health and his family.

Questions/Issues

(1) What are the most significant similarities in the ways the Qur'an and the Bible present Job/Ayyūb?
(2) What are the most significant differences in how they present him?
(3) Does Job/Ayyūb serve as an example and a reminder in the Bible, like he does in the Qur'an?

Further Reading

Johns, A. H. "Narrative, Intertext and Allusion in the Qur'ānic Presentation of Job," *Journal of Qur'anic Studies* 1 (1999): 1–25.

27

John/Yaḥyā

Qur'an 6:84–90; 21:89–90; 19:2–15; 3:35–41

John/Yaḥyā, who is identified as John the Baptist in the New Testament, was the son of Zechariah/Zakarīyā. He is mentioned by name five times in the Qur'an. John/Yaḥyā is explicitly called a prophet in the text, and that role is also implied elsewhere when he is cited in a passage that lists a number of figures who have been given prophetic status (6:84–90). Another text describes his father asking God for a son and after God responds by giving him and his wife John/Yaḥyā, it is said that they all acted rightly, called on God in hope and fear, and lived humble lives (21:89–90). His name likely comes from an Arabic root that means "to make alive," perhaps in reference to his mother's barrenness prior to his birth.

The other two passages that refer to John/Yaḥyā each connect him and his father to the story of the birth of Mary's/Maryam's son Jesus/`Īsā. Both texts describe the circumstances surrounding John's/Yaḥyā's conception before explaining how Jesus/`Īsā was conceived and born. The first (3:35–41) relates how Zechariah/Zakarīyā, who was serving as Mary's/Maryam's caretaker in the temple, asked her about where her food was coming from. When she tells him that it is from God, who provides for all, he immediately asks the deity for a child. Angels then call to him to let him know his prayer has been answered. "God gives you the good news of John, who will confirm a word from God. He will be noble, chaste, and a prophet from among the righteous" (v.39). The reference to John/Yaḥyā confirming a "word from God" is probably an allusion to Jesus/`Īsā, who is sometimes described in this way in the Qur'an, and this is the only verse in the Islamic text that possibly relates to the New Testament theme that John/Yaḥyā was Jesus's/`Īsā's forerunner.

John's/Yaḥyā's conception is also discussed in 19:2–15, where Zechariah/Zakarīyā requests an heir, despite his advanced years and his wife's inability to have a child. God immediately responds that he will have a son whose name will be John/Yaḥyā, a rare honor since Jesus/ʿĪsā is the only other person who is named by God in the Qur'an. This might be hinted at in God's statement that, "We have not given this name to anyone before him" (v.7). The passage ends with a command for John/Yaḥyā to take the Torah as a guide, and then lists his admirable qualities. "'John, hold on to the book with strength!' We gave him wisdom as a child, and tenderness and purity from Us. He was devout and kind to his parents, not proud or disobedient. May peace be upon him the day he was born, the day he dies, and the day he is raised up alive" (vv.12–15). Later in the same chapter Jesus/ʿĪsā will repeat the last sentence in reference to himself, which establishes another connection between the two in the Qur'an (19:33). The Qur'an does not claim that there was a biological relationship between John/Yaḥyā and Jesus/ʿĪsā, as asserted in the Gospel according to Luke (1:36), nor does it offer any details about how John/Yaḥyā died.

In "The Stories of the Prophets," Ibn Kathīr mentions John's/Yaḥyā's serious nature as a child and his wisdom as an adult. He also reports that John/Yaḥyā wept frequently and lived in a grave for a time to remind himself of the shortness of life. In addition, he relates a tradition similar to the one in the New Testament that John/Yaḥyā lost his life when he was beheaded by King Herod.

Questions/Issues

(1) Are the similarities and or the differences more obvious in how John/Yaḥyā is portrayed in the Islamic sources and the New Testament?
(2) How else can the statement that John/Yaḥyā confirmed a word from God be interpreted besides it being an allusion to Jesus/ʿĪsā?
(3) Are there any other ways to understand God's statement regarding John/Yaḥyā that, "We have not given this name to anyone before him"?

Further Reading

Hämeen-Anttila, Jaakko. "John the Baptist and Early Islamic Polemics Concerning Jesus," *Acta Orientalia* 60 (1999), 72–87.

28

Jonah/Yūnus

Qur'an 6:84–86; 4:163; 10:98; 21:87–88; 68:48–50; 37:139–48

The prophet Jonah/Yūnus, whose name provides the title for the tenth chapter of the Qur'an, is mentioned five times in the text. He is also referred to as "the one of the fish" (Arabic, *dhu al-nūn*) and "the companion of the fish" (*ṣāḥib al-ḥūt*). In 6:84–86 Jonah/Yūnus is listed as one among eighteen prophets, all of them biblical figures, who have been chosen and favored by God. Elsewhere he is mentioned as one of a group of individuals, including Muhammad, who received revelation from God (4:163). In another verse, the people of Jonah/Yūnus are singled out as the only ones whose faith was able to save them from the divine wrath. "Why is it that no town believed and benefited from its belief except for the people of Jonah? When they did believe, We took away from them the punishment of disgrace in this world and We gave them enjoyment for a while" (10:98). Unlike in the Bible, where they are the inhabitants of the city of Nineveh, the name and location of Jonah's/Yūnus's people are not identified in the Qur'an.

One passage describes "the one of the fish" angrily departing and assuming that God has no authority over him. He then calls out in the darkness and acknowledges his mistake, at which point the deity answers him and saves him from his distress (21:87–88). His identification as "the one of the fish" in this text, and the reference to him calling out in darkness suggest that this might be related to the biblical scene in which Jonah/Yūnus is swallowed by a great fish that has been sent by God after the prophet attempts to avoid his commission to go to the Ninevites (Jon. 1:17–2:10). In both texts he utters a prayer, with the one in the Bible the longer of the two, and God then rescues him. Despite their brevity, Jonah's/Yūnus's words in the Qur'an contain both a succinct statement of the Islamic understanding of God and the prophet's recognition of his own shortcomings. "There is no god but You. Glory be to You! I am truly an evildoer."

There is another likely allusion to this scene in 68:48–50, where Jonah/Yūnus is not identified by name but is referred to as "the companion of the fish." In this case, as elsewhere in the Qur'an, Muhammad is the addressee and the memory of an earlier figure is invoked so that he might learn from the experiences of his prophetic predecessor. Muhammad is told to be patient and not be like Jonah/Yūnus, who pleaded with God while choking in his distress and would not have been rescued if the deity had not shown him mercy. Muhammad is urged to have the trust and confidence in God that Jonah/Yūnus lacked. In this way, Jonah/Yūnus is unlike other prophets in the Qur'an in that his inability to be faithful to God's call is mentioned in the text.

The Qur'an's longest passage on Jonah/Yūnus is found in 37:139–48, which follows the general outline of the biblical book that bears his name, while lacking its narrative detail. He is sent by God, but tries to run away from that call by fleeing to a ship. Lots are cast, and Jonah/Yūnus is swallowed by a large fish due to his offense. Because he gave glory to God (perhaps a reference to his prayer inside the fish that is quoted in 21:87–88), he is rescued when the deity has the fish spew him out onto dry land. God then causes a gourd tree to grow over Jonah/Yūnus, and the passage concludes by explaining how the people to whom the prophet had been sent, more than one hundred thousand in number, became believers.

"The Stories of the Prophets" and exegetical literature debate Jonah's/Yūnus's perceived sin by which he disobeyed God and left Nineveh angry at him. Some scholars even asserted that Jonah/Yūnus left Nineveh before he was called as a prophet, thus still preserving the idea that the prophets were sinless (al-Rāzī). Moreover, a discussion ensued over whether Jonah/Yūnus was angry with God for not supporting him in his mission or with his people for not being receptive to his call.

Similarly, the Islamic tradition deliberates over how to incorporate biblically inspired traditions. One such tradition narrates that when the gourd plant dried up Jonah/Yūnus began to cry, leading God to ask a question similar to the one that ends the biblical book. "Do you weep over the dry tree, and not weep over the one hundred thousand or more people whom you wanted Me to destroy?" Some commentators appreciated this tradition in that it shows the mistake and lack of compassion of Jonah/Yūnus (al-Thaʿlabī). However, others believed that God would not chastise Jonah/Yūnus in such a way, but would rather gently order him back to his people.

Despite Jonah's/Yūnus's mistake, many *ḥadīth*-based exegetes highlight the prophetic tradition in which Muhammad declares, "It is not permissible for a servant to say, 'I am better than Yūnus b. Matta (Jonah), he praised (*sabbaḥa*) God in the darkness'" (Ibn Kathīr). These exegetes choose to highlight that Jonah/Yūnus praised God in a time of distress and was known to be a righteous servant. God remembered Jonah/Yūnus in a time of need, just as Jonah/Yūnus remembered God in times of ease. In summary, even though Jonah/Yūnus is not seen as one of the steadfast prophets (*ūlū l-ʿazm*), in the Islamic tradition he remains a model for those who acknowledge their mistakes, praise God, and return to him in repentance.

Questions/Issues

(1) Compare the biblical book of Jonah/Yūnus with what is described in the Qur'an in 37:139–48. What are the most significant similarities and differences between the two texts?
(2) How does Islam's overall presentation of the character of Jonah/Yūnus relate to how he is described in the Bible?
(3) Why does the Qur'an include Jonah/Yūnus among the prophets despite his reluctance to do what God wants him to do?
(4) How does Jonah/Yūnus become a model for Muhammad and the Muslim community?

Further Reading

Busse, Heribert. "Jonah," in *Encyclopaedia of the Qurʾān*, ed. Jane Dammen McAuliffe (Leiden: Brill, 2002).

Gregg, Robert C. *Shared Stories, Rival Tellings: Early Encounters of Jews, Christians, and Muslims* (Oxford: Oxford University Press, 2015), pp. 408–54.

Mirza, Younus Y. "Was Ibn Kathir the Spokesperson for Ibn Taymiyya? Jonah as a Prophet of Obedience," *Journal of Qur'anic Studies* 16/1 (2014): 1–19.

29

Joseph/Yūsuf

Qur'an 6:84–87; 40:34; 12:1–111

The twelfth chapter of the Qur'an relates the story of Joseph/Yūsuf, which is the longest single narrative in the entire text. It describes how his brothers betrayed him by sending him to Egypt, where Joseph/Yūsuf rose to a prominent position and was eventually reunited with his family when they journeyed there seeking relief from a famine. He is mentioned by name in two other places, including one passage in which he is listed among a group of important figures from the past (6:84–87). The other verse that treats Joseph/Yūsuf indirectly references the events of his story in chapter 12. "Joseph earlier brought clear proofs to you, but you continued to doubt what he had brought you. Then when he passed away you said, 'God will not send a messenger after him.' This is how God leads astray those who transgress and doubt" (40:34).

The Qur'an's story of Joseph/Yūsuf follows the same general outline as what is reported in Genesis 37–50, but it does not contain the material about Judah and Tamar in Genesis 38 that breaks the flow of the biblical narrative. In the summary of the story that follows, the focus will be on some of the ways that the Islamic version differs from the biblical one, resulting in a tale that is both similar to and different from what is found in Genesis.

Unlike in the Bible, where he relates two dreams he has had to his father Jacob/Ya`qūb and his brothers (Gen. 37:5–11), in the Qur'an Joseph/Yūsuf has just one dream that he describes to his father (vv.4–6). His brothers, who are nameless in the Qur'an, are jealous of Joseph/Yūsuf because he is their father's favorite, but that preference is not expressed through the gift of the coat that Jacob/Ya`qūb gives him in Genesis (37:3). In both stories his brothers throw Joseph/Yūsuf into a well and he is picked up by a passing caravan, but only in the Qur'an does God speak to him and tell him that all will work out in the end. "You will surely tell them of this deed of theirs when they are not aware (of who you are)" (v.15; cf. Gen. 37:18–24). God's presence and knowledge is a theme that resurfaces throughout the Qur'an story, as seen a few verses later when it is stated that God knew what Joseph's/Yūsuf's rescuers did (v.19). The knowledge that Jacob/Ya`qūb possesses is also highlighted in places, as when he appears to predict what will happen to Joseph/Yūsuf (v.13), and in his ability to see through the brothers' false story that Joseph/Yūsuf had been killed by a wild animal. "They came to him with fake blood on his shirt. He said to them, 'No! Rather, your minds have caused you to make up this story. Beautiful patience! God is the one whose help is sought against what you have described' " (v.18).

In both texts Joseph/Yūsuf is sold to an Egyptian man in whose house he works, and the Qur'an makes it clear that God is the one responsible for this development. "Thus did We establish Joseph in the land so that We might teach him about the interpretation of dreams. God is in control of His affairs, but most people do not know" (v.21b). As in Genesis, Joseph's/Yūsuf's master's wife attempts to seduce him, but the details of the episode differ in the two versions (Gen. 39). In the Qur'an's account, God plays a more direct role in enabling Joseph/Yūsuf to not give in to temptation, and the woman's husband returns home just as Joseph/Yūsuf attempts to flee from her after she has torn off a piece of his shirt (vv.23–24). They both protest their innocence, and the man gets at the truth by following the advice of another member of his household to determine which part of the shirt is torn. Seeing that the shirt has been ripped from behind, he identifies his wife as the guilty party and tells her to ask forgiveness for her sin (v.29).

The scene that follows is not in Genesis, but it is mentioned in Jewish sources outside the Bible. When local women chide her because of her infatuation with Joseph/Yūsuf, his master's wife invites them to a meal at her home. When Joseph/Yūsuf enters the room, the women cut themselves with the knives they are holding in their hands because they are overcome by his good looks and they think he is an angel. The master's wife then acknowledges that this is the one she attempted to seduce, and she informs them that she intends to continue to pursue him until he either gives in to her wishes or is imprisoned. The episode ends with God responding favorably to Joseph's/Yūsuf's prayer for strength in the face of temptation (vv.30–34). A number of different versions of the women's meal are found in rabbinic sources, and those texts share common elements with the Qur'an's description of the gathering.

In both the Bible and the Qur'an, Joseph/Yūsuf encounters two fellow prisoners in jail who had been servants of the Egyptian ruler, who is identified as a king rather than a pharaoh in the Islamic text (vv.36–42; cf. Gen. 40). Each man has had a dream that they ask Joseph/Yūsuf to interpret, and as in Genesis he explains that one of them will be freed while the other will be put to death. Prior to the interpretation of the dreams, the Qur'an includes a short speech by Joseph/Yūsuf in which he tells them about the nature of true belief.

> I follow the religion of my fathers Abraham, Isaac, and Jacob. We do not associate anything with God ... Oh my fellow prisoners, are many gods better than God the one, the all-powerful? What you worship apart from Him are nothing but names that you and your fathers have given. God has revealed no authority for them. Judgment belongs only to God. He commands that you worship none but Him. That is the proper faith, but most people do not know. (vv.37–40)

With these words, Joseph/Yūsuf echoes the prophets who have come before him, and he anticipates the teaching of those yet to come, including Muhammad. In this way, as with many of the other prophets it mentions, the Qur'an's presentation of Joseph/Yūsuf serves to legitimate the core message of Islam. Another element of the Qur'an's telling of the story that does not have a counterpart in the Bible is a reference to Satan/Shayṭān as the one responsible for Joseph's/Yūsuf's extended stay in prison. "He said to the one he knew would be released, 'Mention me to your master.' But Satan caused him to forget to mention him to his master, so he (Joseph) remained in prison for some years" (v.42; cf. v.100).

Joseph's/Yūsuf's release from prison in both texts is tied to his ability to interpret the Egyptian ruler's dreams about a coming famine, but in the Qur'an he gives the interpretation to the prisoner who had been freed rather than to the king himself (vv.43–49; cf. Gen. 41:1–36). This is followed by a passage in which he is exonerated after his master's wife admits to the Egyptian leader that she had tried to seduce Joseph/Yūsuf, a scene not in Genesis (vv.50–53). The king then sets Joseph/Yūsuf over all the storehouses of the land in anticipation of the famine, a development that the Qur'an understands to be an act of God "Thus We established Joseph in the land, and he lived there as he pleased" (vv.54–57).

Genesis and the Qur'an describe how his brothers come to Joseph/Yūsuf in Egypt seeking relief from the famine, but they fail to recognize him. In both texts he orders them to return home and bring back their younger brother, who is named Benjamin in the Bible. In the biblical story Joseph/Yūsuf guarantees their return by imprisoning one of the brothers (Gen. 42:6–17), and in the Qur'an he does so by withholding grain from them until they come back with their brother (vv.58–60). Jacob/Ya`qūb is hesitant to allow his youngest son to make the journey to Egypt, but in both texts he relents and places him in his brothers' care. Prior to their departure Jacob/Ya`qūb asks that God be with his sons when they encounter Joseph/Yūsuf again (Gen. 43:14), but in the Qur'an three times during his conversation with them prior to their departure Jacob/Ya`qūb expresses faith in God. "He replied, 'Shall I trust you with him as I trusted you previously with his brother? God is the best guardian and the most merciful'" (v.64; cf. vv.66, 67).

Joseph/Yūsuf is reduced to tears twice in the Bible when he encounters his brothers, including once when he first sees Benjamin (Gen. 43:30–31; cf. Gen. 42:22–24), but he does not display this level of emotion in the Qur'an. Joseph's/Yūsuf's revelation of his true identity is described differently in the two texts because he immediately tells Benjamin who he is in a private conversation, whereas he informs the other brothers much later. "When they entered Joseph's presence he showed hospitality to his brother and said, 'I am your brother, so do not be troubled by what they have been doing'" (v.69). As in Genesis, a royal cup is planted among Benjamin's belongings so that he might be accused of being a thief. In the Bible, Judah then delivers a speech that centers on how much Jacob/Ya`qūb has suffered in the years since Joseph/Yūsuf was "killed," causing Joseph/Yūsuf to reveal his true identity to all of the brothers at once (Gen. 44:1–45:3). The Qur'an includes a plot wrinkle whereby Benjamin is imprisoned for his offense and most of the other brothers return to Jacob/Ya`qūb, who continues to place his trust in God and suggests that Joseph/Yūsuf might in fact still be alive. "Oh my sons, go and inquire about Joseph and his brother, and do not despair of God's spirit. None despair of God's spirit except the unbelievers" (v.87). They obey their father's command and return to Egypt, and at that point Joseph/Yūsuf reveals his true identity to them (v.88–92).

Joseph/Yūsuf is reunited with his entire family at the end of the story, including his father Jacob/Ya`qūb, whom he cures of blindness (vv.84, 93, 96). Also mentioned for the first time in the Qur'an is his unnamed mother (vv.99–100), who died in childbirth when Benjamin was born in the Genesis version and so does not play a role in the biblical story of Joseph/Yūsuf (Gen. 35:16–20). As his tale draws to a close, Joseph/Yūsuf addresses his family members and refers to God in ways that cohere with the Islamic understanding of the deity. When his brothers state that God has preferred Joseph/Yūsuf over them and they admit their sins against him, he reminds them of the deity's compassionate nature. "No blame shall come upon you this day. May God forgive you—He is the most merciful of all" (v.92). Joseph's/Yūsuf's final words in the story are directed to his father, and in them he expresses his belief that God was behind all that happened in his life and he identifies himself as a *muslim* who submits to the divine will at all times.

> Oh my father, this is the meaning of my earlier vision. My Lord has made it come true. He favored me when He removed me from prison, and He brought you out of the desert after Satan had sown discord between me and my brothers. Truly,

> He is kind to whomever He wishes, for He is the one who knows and the one who is wise. Oh my Lord, You have given me authority and You have taught me how to interpret events. Creator of heaven and earth, You are my guardian in the world and in the hereafter. Let me die a submitter, and join me to the righteous ones. (vv.100–1)

"The Stories of the Prophets" literature provides details about the life of Joseph/Yūsuf that are not in the Qur'an. Rachel is identified as Joseph's/Yūsuf's mother, and names are given to some of the other figures, including several of his brothers and his Egyptian master and his wife (Potiphar and Zuleikha). At a young age Joseph/Yūsuf was given a coat, in addition to four other items that were handed down to him from Abrham/Ibrāhīm. When Joseph/Yūsuf was thrown into the well by his brothers, God does not speak to him as in the Qur'an, but the angel Gabriel/Jibrīl comes to assist him.

Once the story's location shifts to Egypt, "The Stories of the Prophets" recount a tradition about how Joseph/Yūsuf was dressed up in fine clothes for a slave auction and was sold for a high price. Upon arriving in Egypt, Joseph/Yūsuf meets a man from his homeland who knows his father Jacob/Ya`qūb, and he promises to tell him that Joseph/Yūsuf is alive and safe when he returns to Canaan. The man does so, but Jacob/Ya`qūb does not mention this encounter again in the rest of the story. The seduction scene that the sources relate is similar to that of the Qur'an, but when Joseph/Yūsuf is sent to prison the account diverges from the Qur'an's when he is again visited by Gabriel/Jibrīl. When Joseph/Yūsuf is released from prison one of the people who come to him seeking provisions is his Egyptian master's wife Zuleikha, who is now a widow. She and Joseph/Yūsuf get married and they remain together until the end of the account, when she precedes him in death.

The description in "The Stories of the Prophets" of how Joseph/Yūsuf is reunited with his family is fairly close to that of the Qur'an, but with some additional information included. His full brother Benjamin has three sons who are named "Wolf," "Blood," and "Joseph," in memory of the way in which Joseph/Yūsuf was taken from him. When the brothers return to Jacob/Ya`qūb from Egypt without Benjamin and Judah, he is comforted by God and told that he will be reunited with Joseph/Yūsuf. In the scene in which Joseph/Yūsuf reveals his true identity to his brothers, he shows them two things not mentioned in the Qur'an—the piece of paper containing the record of the transaction when he was sold into Egypt, and a mark on his head that is similar to one on the head of their father Jacob/Ya`qūb. (al-Kisā'ī)

Questions/Issues

(1) Choose one of the scenes in the Joseph/Yūsuf story that is found in both texts and do a close analysis of it that highlights the similarities and differences in how it is presented in the Bible and the Qur'an.

(2) How can we explain the fact that the scene that depicts the women's meal in which they cut themselves with knives is found in the Qur'an and rabbinic sources, but is not in the Bible?

(3) Compare how the character of God functions in the story of Joseph/Yūsuf as told in Genesis and the Islamic sources.

Further Reading

Afsar, Ayaz. "Plot Motifs in Joseph/Yūsuf Story: A Comparative Study of Biblical and Qur'ānic Narrative," *Islamic Studies* 45/2 (2006), 167–89

Bernstein, Marc. "The Story of Our Master Joseph: The Spiritual or the Righteous," in *Judaism and Islam: Boundaries, Communications, and Interaction: Essays in Honor of William M. Brinner*, ed. Benjamin H. Hary, John L. Hayes and Fred Astren (Leiden; Boston: Brill, 2000): pp. 157–67.

Haleem, M. A. Abdel. "The Story of Joseph in the Qur'an and the Old Testament," *Islam and Christian-Muslim Relations* 1/2 (1990), 171–91.

Kaltner, John. *Inquiring of Joseph: Getting to Know a Biblical Character through the Qur'an* (Collegeville: Liturgical Press, 2003).

Waldman, Marilyn. "New Approaches to 'Biblical' Materials in the Qur'an," *The Muslim World* 75/1 (1985), 1–16.

30

Korah/Qārūn

Qur'an 28:76–82; 29:39–40; 40:23–24

Korah/Qārūn is cited by name three times in the Qur'an, and in two of those texts he is mentioned along with Pharaoh/Fir`awn and Haman/Hāmān as enemies of Moses/Mūsā. In 40:23–24 the three of them call him a liar, and in 29:39–40 they are described as arrogant individuals who will be held accountable for their actions. The latter passage lists a series of punishments that God inflicted on them, but it does not identify which individual received which punishment. The third Qur'an text that refers to Korah/Qārūn leaves no doubt that he is the one who was punished by having the earth swallow him alive.

The main Qur'an passage involving Korah/Qārūn is found in 28:76–82, which presents him as one of Moses's/Mūsā's people who treated others unfairly. He was a person whose great wealth had been given to him by God, but he attributed his success to his own wisdom and knowledge. This causes some of the other people of Moses/Mūsā to describe him as a gloater (v.76) and a creator of corruption (v.77), which causes division with the community. As Korah/Qārūn struts about in his fancy attire, some of his contemporaries jealously long to be like him, while others reject what he stands for in their belief that reward comes to those who are faithful and act righteously. The former group are referred to as "those who desire this world," and the latter are "those who have been given knowledge" (vv.79–80). God then causes the earth to swallow up Korah/Qārūn and his entire house without warning, which causes those who had wished to be like him to realize the error of their ways.

The biblical story of Korah/Qārūn is found in the book of Numbers (16:1–35), and it is set in the wilderness wanderings after the Israelites have escaped from Egypt in the Exodus. He is described as a member of the tribe of Levi who is jealous of Moses/Mūsā and Aaron/ Hārūn and is obsessed with acquiring more power. Moses/Mūsā plays a major role in the biblical account, which is primarily a story about his and Aaron's/ Hārūn's legitimacy as leaders of the community. In the Qur'an, though, Moses/Mūsā is a marginal figure in the material about Korah/Qārūn—he is not even mentioned in the story about him being swallowed by the earth—and Aaron/ Hārūn is completely missing. Another difference between the two versions is that the Bible does not call attention to Korah's/ Qārūn's great wealth, which is a significant element of the Qur'an story. The Bible also does not make any connection between Korah/Qārūn and Pharaoh/ Fir'awn or Haman/Hāmān.

Questions/Issues

(1) How do the differences in the ways Korah/Qārūn is presented in the Bible and the Qur'an influence the way his character is viewed in the two texts?
(2) Identify and compare the main point or lesson of the story of Korah/ Qārūn as it is told in both the Qur'an and the Bible.
(3) Why might it be that Moses/Mūsā plays less of a role in the traditions about Korah/Qārūn in the Qur'an than he does in the Bible?

31

Lot/Lūṭ

Qur'an 11:69–83; 15:51–77; 29:31–35; 7:80–84; 26:160–74; 27:54–58; 37:133–38; 54:33–37; 21:74; 4:15–16

Lot/Lūṭ is a prophet and messenger referred to by name twenty-seven times in the Qur'an. The majority of those references are found in passages that describe the punishment of his people for their sinful actions. Only the punishment of the people of Noah/Nūḥ is mentioned more frequently in the text. Although he is not explicitly described as a relative of Abraham/Ibrāhīm in the Qur'an as he is in the Bible, several passages mirror the order of the events in Genesis 18–19 by having the story of Lot/Lūṭ follow the visit of God's messengers to Abraham/Ibrāhīm to announce the birth of Isaac/Isḥāq (11:69–83; 15:51–77; 29:31–35). More commonly, the tradition about the destruction of Lot's/Lūṭ's city is found on its own without being linked to Abraham/Ibrāhīm (7:80–84; 26:160–74; 27:54–58; 37:133–38; 54:33–37).

The general outline of the Qur'an's descriptions of the punishment of Lot's/Lūṭ's people is similar to that of Genesis 19, although not every element of the biblical plot is found in each of the Qur'an's versions. Lot/Lūṭ criticizes them for their desire to mistreat God's messengers, who are his houseguests, and he offers them his daughters as an alternative. They reject that offer and attempt to force their way into his house, but God prevents them from doing so by blinding them. Lot/Lūṭ and his family are instructed to flee at night, and the city (unnamed in the Qur'an) is destroyed in the morning. Most of the passages report that Lot's/Lūṭ's wife remained behind and was killed along with the other inhabitants.

The Qur'an is consistent in its negative depiction of the people of the city. "As for Lot, We gave him good judgment and knowledge. We delivered him from the town that was engaging in lewdness. Truly, they were an evil, vile people" (21:74). Their actions are described in several places with the Arabic term *fāḥishah*, which can refer to any immoral or indecent act (7:80; 27:54; 29:28).

Several passages specify their offense as the men's sexual desire or lust for other men. In this verse, Lot/Lūṭ chastises the men of his town, "Of all humankind, do you come to the males and reject the spouses God has created for you? You are a people who exceed the bounds!" (26:165–66; cf. 7:81; 27:55). These are the Qur'an's only explicit references to same-sex attraction, but some scholars have suggested that there may be another allusion to it in 4:15–16.

The punishment that God visits on the people of Lot/Lūṭ is described in several different ways in the Qur'an. A few passages speak in general terms about something raining from the sky (7:84; 26:173; 27:58), and elsewhere it is specified that baked clay stones fall from the heavens (11:82; 15:74). Another chapter describes it as a stormy wind of stones that causes them to lose their eyesight (54:34–37).

"The Stories of the Prophets" literature adds various details regarding the sins of the people of Lot/Lūṭ and the confrontation between him and them. Besides same-sex desire, their offense is also identified as raiding, deception, and bad speech (Ibn Kathīr). Some note that the people of Lot/Lūṭ would raid the caravans of their guests and then rape them (al-Kisā'ī). The literature also describes how the angels approached the city and eventually found themselves in Lot's/Lūṭ's house. Some sources highlight the differences between the biblical and Qur'anic versions by pointing out that in the Bible there are only two angels and that they have a meal with Lot/Lūṭ (Ibn Kathīr).

"The Stories of the Prophets" also relate the dramatic scene in which Lot's/Lūṭ's people storm his house and demand that he turn over his guests. When Lot/Lūṭ learns that his people are approaching, he immediately closes and locks the door. The townsmen are not deterred, and they begin to bang on the door and eventually break it down. The commentators then try to explain why Lot/Lūṭ offered his daughters to his guests. Many interpret the act metaphorically, by stating that Lot/Lūṭ was encouraging his people to marry the daughters of the town since the prophets and their wives are like the fathers and mothers of their people. The Qur'an, for instance, speaks about the wives of the prophets as the "mothers of the believers" (Ibn Kathīr).

After the townsmen refuse Lot's/Lūṭ's offer, he stands in front of the door where the guests are hiding and defends them by saying, "I will not hand my guests over to you! Not over my dead body!" A man from the people approaches Lot/Lūṭ, slaps him in his face, and tries to throw him to the ground. The mob then surrounds Lot/Lūṭ, grabs his beard, and pushes him away from the guests. Lot/Lūṭ then utters a prayer that is found in the Qur'an (11:80). "If only I had the strength to stop you or could rely on strong support!" The guests then identify themselves as angels, and they begin to defend Lot/Lūṭ as Gabriel/Jibrīl is transformed from a human being to an angel, spreads out his wings, and blinds the people (al-Kisā'ī). Unable to see, the townspeople wander in the streets and are unable to find their way back home. They begin to warn others that there were sorcerers in Lot's/Lūṭ's house, and they then threaten him for what he had done to them (al-Tha'labī). Now realizing that the guests are angels who have come to destroy the city, Lot/Lūṭ asks them when the punishment will occur. They respond that it will arrive in the morning and that they must leave that night. The literature goes on to discuss in detail how the people of Lot/Lūṭ were punished, with many noting that Gabriel/Jibrīl destroyed the city by attacking it with his wings. Everyone in the city perished except for the few believers who were able to leave with Lot/Lūṭ. Thus, "The Stories of the Prophets" literature adds to the list of the evils committed by Lot's/Lūṭ's people, and it dramatizes his confrontation with them.

Questions/Issues

(1) What are the most significant differences between the description of the destruction of Sodom and Gomorrah in Genesis 19 and the Qur'an's accounts of the event?
(2) Some Bible scholars have suggested that Sodom and Gomorrah were punished for violating the rules of hospitality, rather than for reasons related to homosexuality. Can the Qur'an passages be interpreted in the same way?
(3) List the main similarities and differences in how Lot/Lūṭ is presented in the Bible and the Islamic sources.

Further Reading

Leemhuis, Fred. "Lūt and His People in the Koran and Its Early Commentaries," in *Sodom's Sin: Genesis 18–19 and Its Interpretations* ed. Ed Noort and Eibert J. C. Tigchelaar (Leiden: Brill, 2004), pp. 97–115.

32

Lot's/Lūṭ's Wife

Qur'an 7:83; 15:58–60; 26:171; 27:57; 29:32–33; 37:135; 11:81; 15:58–60; 66:10

The wife of Lot/Lūṭ is mentioned in eight different chapters in the Qur'an, and in every case but one she is identified as the only member of his family who did not escape the destruction of their city. In most of those passages she is referred to as one of those who "stayed behind" (7:83; 15:58–60; 26:171; 27:57; 29:32–33; 37:35). In two verses she is described as an old woman and is not called Lot's/Lūṭ's spouse (26:171; 37:135). The reason for her staying behind is not explicitly stated in the text, but in several places it is decreed by God (or his messengers) that she will not go with the rest of her family (11:81; 15:58–60; 27:57). One of those passages seems to imply that she is a sinner when God's messengers inform Abraham/Ibrāhīm, "We have been sent to a people who are sinners, except for Lot's house. We will truly save all of them except his wife, because we have decreed that she will be one of those who stay behind" (15:58–60).

One text is different from the others in that it links her with the wife of Noah/Nūḥ as two unbelieving women who were punished in hell.

> God has given an example for those who disbelieve—the wife of Noah and the wife of Lot. They came under Our two righteous servants, but they betrayed them. They (Noah and Lot) were not of any use to them against God, and so it was said to both of them, "Enter the fire with the others who enter it." (66:10)

This verse suggests that the wives of Noah/Nūḥ and Lot/Lūṭ were somehow disloyal to their husbands or refused to heed the prophets' messages from God, and were therefore punished for their offenses. Nowhere else does the Qur'an explain or describe what the two women did to be punished in this manner.

The passages that understand her staying behind as predetermined by God offer a perspective on her character that differs from the way she is presented in the Bible. In Genesis 19, she disobeys a divine command to not turn around and she looks at Sodom and Gomorrah as they are being destroyed, but in the Qur'an her remaining in the city is part of God's plan. In both texts she loses her life, but the reasons for her demise differ considerably. In the Bible, the wife of Lot/Lūṭ dies because she refuses to accept the divine will, while in the Qur'an her death is an act of submission to that will.

"The Stories of the Prophets" literature describes the wife of Lot/Lūṭ as a traitor and one who preferred her people over her husband and God. When the angels in the shape of men are safely escorted to Lot's/Lūṭ's house, she sneaks away and informs her people of their presence and tells them how beautiful the angels are (al-Ṭarafī). Some explain that this was a consistent act on her part in that she frequently notified the people of the town when Lot/Lūṭ had guests. When a visitor would come to Lot's/Lūṭ's house during the day, she would send up a smoke signal, and when they came at night she would light a fire (al-Kisāʾī). The literature further debates whether she left with her family when the city was being destroyed, or if she stayed within the city. One story narrates that she left with Lot/Lūṭ, but when she heard the punishment beginning she violated the divine order by turning back and she was destroyed (Ibn Kathīr). The literature also debates the nature of her disobedience; was she simply disagreeing with her husband, or did she disobey a prophet's commands? "The Stories of the Prophets" literature prefers the latter alternative by claiming that she helped her people storm the house of Lot/Lūṭ when they tried to take his guest away from him (Ibn Kathīr). In this way, these sources condemn the wife of Lot/Lūṭ for showing more loyalty to her people than to either her husband or God.

Questions/Issues

(1) Is the wife of Lot/Lūṭ a more positive character in Islam than she is in the Bible?

(2) Do you think the Qur'an's reference to her in 15:58–60 presents Lot's/Lūṭ's wife as a sinner, or can that passage be interpreted in some other way?

(3) Is it possible to interpret the biblical story in Genesis 19 in a way that agrees with the Islamic sources by saying that the wife of Lot/Lūṭ aligned herself with the people of her city rather than with Lot/Lūṭ and God?

33

Mary/Maryam

Qur'an 66:12; 21:91; 23:50; 12:109; 16:43; 3:35–47; 19:16–29

Mary/Maryam is the only woman mentioned by name in the entire Qur'an, where she is referred to specifically thirty-four times in the text. Twenty-three of those occurrences simply define her as the mother of Jesus/`Īsā and do not provide any information about her. Of the remaining eleven references, six of them are found in the account of her birth and the announcement of her pregnancy that are related in 3:35–47. Chapter 19 of the Qur'an, which contains another passage that speaks of the birth of Jesus/`Īsā, is named after Mary/Maryam.

In 66:12, Mary's/Maryam's modesty and obedience are underscored, which are central themes of the Qur'an's presentation of her. The verse prior to that links her with the wife of Pharaoh/Fir`awn as two women who serve as models for all believers. Two other passages do not mention Mary/Maryam by name, but they describe her and Jesus/`Īsā as signs for others. "We breathed some of Our spirit into the one who guarded her private parts, and We made her and her son a sign to the worlds" (21:91; cf. 23:50). This verse is found in a chapter that is titled "The Prophets," and it mentions by name eighteen other individuals who are all recognized as prophets in Islam. This raises the question of whether or not Mary/Maryam should be included among their ranks and be identified as a prophet. Very few Muslim commentators have entertained that possibility, primarily because certain texts in the Qur'an have been interpreted in a way that limits prophetic status to males only (see, for example, 12:109 and 16:43). Nonetheless, as discussed below, Mary's/Maryam's story in the Qur'an contains some provocative connections with those of some of the prophets mentioned elsewhere in the book.

As suggested in 21:91, the Qur'an teaches that Jesus/`Īsā was virginally conceived by Mary/Maryam in agreement with what is found in the New Testament Gospels of Matthew (1:18–25) and Luke (1:26–38). Two versions of the annunciation to Mary/Maryam about her pregnancy are found in the Islamic text, and there are certain narrative differences between them. The first is found at 3:35–47, which opens with the Qur'an's only reference to Mary's/Maryam's birth, a topic not discussed at all in the New Testament. Her father is identified as `Imrān, and her mother dedicates her to God's service and seeks divine protection for Mary/Maryam and her offspring prior to her birth (3:35–36).

The next five verses show the realization of the mother's prayer as Mary's/Maryam's dedication to God is described and the divine protection she receives is made evident. Zechariah/Zakarīyā, the father of John/Yaḥyā (identified as John the Baptist in the New Testament), is her caretaker as Mary/Maryam resides in the shrine or temple where she serves God. Despite his best efforts to take care of her, Zechariah/Zakarīyā is preempted by the deity whenever he tries to tend to Mary's/Maryam's needs.

> So her Lord accepted her graciously. He caused her to grow up well, and gave her into the care of Zechariah. Every time Zechariah came to see her in the chamber he found her with provisions. He said, "Oh Mary, where did you get this?" She answered, "It is from God. Truly, God provides for whomever He wishes without measure." (3:37)

This causes Zechariah/Zakarīyā to immediately call upon God and request a child despite his and his wife's advanced years and inability to conceive. His petition is then answered by angels, who inform him that John/Yaḥyā will be born. In this way, the provisions that Mary/Maryam receives serve a double function—they are both an expression of the protection God gives her and a means by which Zechariah/Zakarīyā is also able to get what he needs from the deity. Mary's/Maryam's statement that God provides for everyone becomes the catalyst that enables Zechariah/Zakarīyā to experience divine favor. In effect, the roles have been reversed as she becomes his caretaker.

Zechariah's/Zakarīyā's only appearance in the New Testament is found in the first chapter of the Gospel according to Luke, which is both similar to and different from this Qur'an passage. Most notably, Luke's story is set in the temple in Jerusalem where Zechariah/Zakarīyā is an attendant and Mary/Maryam is not present. In addition, there are interesting similarities between this Qur'an text and the Protoevangelium of James, a non-canonical Christian writing from the second century CE. In that work Zechariah/Zakarīyā is a functionary in the temple and angels miraculously provide Mary/Maryan with sustenance.

After their conversation with Zechariah/Zakarīyā the angels then inform Mary/Maryam of her pregnancy, which causes her to object in a way similar to how she responds in the Gospel according to Luke.

> The angels said, "Oh Mary, God gives you the good news of a word from him. His name will be the Messiah Jesus, the son of Mary, who will be eminent in this world and in the next, and will be one of those brought near. He shall speak to people from the cradle and in his later years, and he will be one of the righteous." She said, "My Lord, how can I have a child when no man has touched me?" He said, "Thus it is. God creates what He wills. If He decrees something, He only need say 'Be' and it is." (3:45–47)

Prior to this, there is a verse directed to Muhammad reminding him that he was not present when lots were cast to see who would take care of Mary/Maryam. This tradition is not found in the New Testament, but it is mentioned in the Protoevangelium of James, when the men of the area engage in a game of chance to see who will be Mary's/Maryam's caretaker. This Qur'an passage clearly maintains that Jesus/`Īsā was virginally conceived, but in keeping with the way he is presented elsewhere in the book the manner of his conception does not elevate him above other human beings and make him divine.

The other text in which Mary/Maryam figures prominently is 19:16–29, which reports both the announcement of her pregnancy and the birth of Jesus/`Īsā but does not mention either Zechariah/Zakarīyā or the birth of John/Yaḥyā. This passage is not set in a temple or shrine, and it begins by describing Mary/Maryam as traveling on her own to some undisclosed location in the east. She is not alone for long because she soon encounters a messenger who the text says is "Our spirit which looked like a human being to her" (19:17), who informs Mary/Maryam that she will have a child. "I am only a messenger from your Lord to give you a righteous son" (19:19). His words could suggest that she becomes pregnant in the usual way, but that is not how commentators have interpreted the passage. The Arabic word for God's spirit (*rūh*) can also mean "breath," and this is the basis for the view that the divine messenger somehow breathed into Mary/Maryam and caused her pregnancy. This idea is supported by what is said in 21:91, which was cited earlier.

The Qur'an's only account of Jesus's/`Īsā's birth follows as Mary/Maryam distances herself further from home and delivers him near a palm tree. At this point, a mysterious voice speaks in an effort to comfort and reassure her. "Do not grieve! Your Lord has placed a stream beneath you. Shake the trunk of the palm tree and it will drop fresh ripe dates on you. Eat, drink, and be consoled. If you should see another person, say, 'I have vowed a fast to the merciful one, and I will not speak to anyone today'" (19:24–25). The identity of the speaker is not given, and some commentators say it was the divine messenger, while others claim it was the newborn Jesus/`Īsā. An argument in favor of the latter alternative is that the text specifies that the voice came from below Mary/Maryam, and so a common interpretation suggests that his ability to speak as soon as he left the womb was the first miracle that Jesus/`Īsā performed.

The idea that Jesus/`Īsā is the speaker is supported by what happens next, when Mary/Maryam returns to her people and receives a chilly welcome. "She carried him (Jesus) to her people, who said, 'Oh Mary, you have done something strange! Oh sister of Aaron, your father was not wicked nor was your mother unchaste.' Then she pointed to him. They said, 'How can we talk to a child in the cradle?' " (19:27–29). Jesus/`Īsā then proceeds to speak with them about who he is and what he will do later in his life. The people's reference to Mary/Maryam as "sister of Aaron" has been explained by commentators in a number of ways. Her name is identical to that of Miriam, who is identified in the Bible as the sister of Moses/Mūsā and Aaron/Hārūn. Rather than seeing this as evidence of the Qur'an's confusion between the two women, some scholars have argued that Mary/Maryam is Aaron's/Hārūn's sister in a symbolic or spiritual sense since they are both believers in God. Others have suggested that Mary/Maryam did in fact have a brother named Aaron/Hārūn, who is otherwise not mentioned in the biblical or Islamic sources.

Mary's/Maryam's rejection by "her people" is one of the aspects of her character in the Qur'an that might be used to argue that she is a prophet, since throughout the text prophets are rejected by their own people when they come bringing God's word. Mary/Maryam follows this pattern in that God communicates with her and gives her his word (3:45), which she then brings to her people who have a difficult time accepting it. In addition, the traditional identification of the angel who spoke to her as Gabriel/Jibrīl, the same messenger who brought the Qur'an to Muhammad, provides another intriguing connection between Mary/Maryam and the prophets. Regardless of where one comes down on the question of her prophetic status, there is no doubt that Mary/Maryam plays a special role in the Qur'an and Islam, as seen in the fact that Muslim theologians and commentators have often numbered her among the most preeminent women who have ever lived.

"The Stories of the Prophets" literature emphasizes the importance of Mary's/Maryam's birth and her status as one of the most pious women of all time. For instance, a prophetic tradition states that "Satan touches every child from the children of Adam with his finger except Mary/Maryam." After Mary/Maryam was born and weaned, her parents immediately put her in the service of the temple where she worshiped and grew close to God. It was said that she prayed so much that her feet began to crack. The commentators also emphasize the fact that God chose her "from all of the women of the world." A debate thus emerged over whether women like Mary/Maryam, the mother of Moses/Mūsā, and Abraham's/Ibrāhīm's wife Sarah could have been prophets because they either received revelation (*waḥy*) or were spoken to by angels. Several traditions are quoted saying that the best of women are Mary/Maryam, Āsiya (the wife of Pharaoh), Khadija (the wife of Muhammad) and Fatima (the daughter of Muhammad).

"The Stories of the Prophets" literature also identifies Gabriel/Jibrīl as the one who came to visit Mary/Maryam and informed her of the impending birth of Jesus/'Īsā. Gabriel/Jibrīl is understood to be the messenger referred to as "Our spirit" in 19:17. The literature also debates whether it was Gabriel/Jibrīl or Jesus/'Īsā who spoke to Mary/Maryam "from below," telling her not to worry when the labor pains began to increase. As noted above, many of the commentators say the voice came from Jesus/'Īsā, and his speaking as an infant was one of his miracles. The scholars also debate the meaning of the phrase "sister of Aaron/Hārūn" as either meaning that Mary/Maryam literally had a brother with that name, or that she was called by the prophets of her family. One tradition states that a companion of the Prophet Muhammad was sent to the Christian empire of Najrān, where they questioned him regarding the verse. On returning to Arabia, the companion asked Muhammad about the meaning of the phrase and he responded, "You should have informed [the people of Najrān] that they used to be called by the prophets and the righteous people before them" (Ibn Kathīr).

The literature also dramatizes Mary's/Maryam's pregnancy and the birth of Jesus/'Īsā. In one story, right before her impending labor Mary/Maryam goes to the house of her aunt, who is the wife of Zechariah/Zakarīyā and the mother of John/Yaḥyā. Her aunt greets Mary/Maryam and then asks, "Do you think that I am pregnant?" Mary/Maryam replies, "Do you think that I am pregnant?" The wife of Zechariah/Zakarīyā then responds, "Verily, I find what is in my stomach prostrating to what is in your stomach." The commentators take this exchange as an explanation of the verse that describes John/Yaḥyā as "confirming a word from God" (3:39) in that he was bowing in respect to Jesus/'Īsā.

In another story, Mary's/Maryam's companion Joseph/Yūsuf, the carpenter, asks her about her pregnancy in a roundabout way. He asks first whether a plant could grow without a seed or a tree could grow without rain. He then asks whether a child could be born without a male. Mary/Maryam explains to Joseph/Yūsuf that God originally created plants without seeds and trees without water. She asks him, "Did he not create Adam and his wife without a male or female?" Joseph/Yūsuf then understood that the pregnancy was something from God (al-Thaʿlabī). In this way, the literature emphasizes the special status of Mary/Maryam and dramatizes the coming birth of Jesus/ʿĪsā.

Questions/Issues

(1) Her husband Joseph is not mentioned in the Qur'an passages that treat Mary/Maryam. How does his absence affect how her character is understood?
(2) Why might it be that no other women besides Mary/Maryam are mentioned by name in the Qur'an?
(3) What are some of the most significant similarities and differences between how Mary/Maryam is presented in the Islamic sources and the New Testament?

Further Reading

Gregg, Robert C. *Shared Stories, Rival Tellings: Early Encounters of Jews, Christians, and Muslims* (Oxford: Oxford University Press, 2015), pp.543–93.
Lybarger, Loren D. "Gender and Prophetic Authority in the Qur'anic Story of Maryam: A Literary Approach," *Journal of Religion* 80 (2000), 240–70.
Mourad, Suleiman A. "Mary in the Qur'an: A Reexamination of Her Presentation," in *The Qur'an in Its Historical Context* ed. Gabriel Said Reynolds (New York: Routledge, 2008), pp. 163–74.

Messengers

Qur'an 16:36; 10:47; 28:59; 14:4; 7:65–72; 26:141–59; 11:84–95; 21:7; 12:109; 16:43; 21:8; 23:31–33; 10:21; 15:57; 51:31; 4:163; 17:55; 40:78a; 4:164; 48:29; 7:158; 33:21; 2:253a; 4:152; 15:11; 23:44; 2:87; 5:70; 22:52

The Arabic term for a messenger is *rasūl* (plural, *rusul*), which appears more than 300 times in the text of the Qur'an. The etymologically related word *mursal* ("one sent with a message") appears approximately thirty-five times. They both describe a human emissary who has been sent by God to a particular people with a clear message. A series of such messengers are mentioned in the text, and the core of each one's message is essentially the same—they urge their audiences to avoid improper worship and to follow the one true God. Their common message is summarized in this verse. "We have indeed sent a messenger to every community saying, 'Serve God and reject false deities!' Among them were some whom God guided, and others whose error was deserved. Travel throughout the earth and notice what happened to the ones who denied the message" (16:36). According to this verse, every group of people has been sent a messenger (cf. 10:47; 28:59), and another passage makes it clear that each messenger spoke in a language that was understood by his audience. "We have sent no messenger except in his people's language, so that he could make (the message) intelligible for them. God leads astray those He wishes, and guides those He wishes. He is the mighty one, the wise one" (14:4).

Many of the messengers cited in the Qur'an are also biblical figures, including Noah/Nūḥ, Lot/Lūṭ, Moses/Mūsā, Elijah/Ilyās, Jonah/Yūnus, and Jesus/`Īsā. Others identified as messengers in the Qur'an are Hūd (7:65–72), Ṣāliḥ (26:141–59), and Shu`ayb (11:84–95), Arabian prophets who lived prior to Muhammad's lifetime. There are traditions from sources outside the Qur'an that speak of southern Arabian tomb inscriptions identifying Hūd and Shu`ayb, among others, as messengers of God.

All of the individuals mentioned above are males, and throughout history the vast majority of Muslim scholars have maintained that the Qur'an limits the office of messenger (and that of prophet) to men only and therefore excludes women from their ranks. This view is based on several verses in the Qur'an that have almost identical wording. "Prior to you (Muhammad), all the messengers we sent were men to whom We had given revelation. If you do not know this, ask the People of the Reminder" (21:7; cf. 12:109; 16:43). The "People of the Reminder" is a reference to Jews and Christians, to whom most of the previous messengers mentioned in the Qur'an had been sent. While these passages have often been read as restricting the roles of messenger and prophet to men only, it should be noted that they do not contain the word denoting a male (as opposed to a female) that is found nearly twenty times in the Qur'an. They rather use a term that can sometimes convey the sense of "human being" without specifying the person's gender. Some commentators have suggested that the distinction that is being made in these verses is not that of male/female, but that of human/nonhuman. In particular, it has been argued that the texts are stating that God has sent human beings, rather than angels, as messengers to deliver divine revelation to communities of people. This reading is supported by the verse that immediately follows the one quoted above, which stresses the humanity of the messengers God has sent. "And We did not make them as bodies that did not eat, nor were they immortal" (21:8; cf. 23:31–33). At the same time, it should be noted that the Qur'an contains several verses in which angels are described as messengers (10:21; 15:57; 51:31).

How the roles of prophet and messenger differ is not completely clear in the Qur'an. A careful reading of the text indicates that all messengers are prophets, but not all prophets are messengers, and so some individuals carry both titles. This can be seen with Moses/Mūsā, Jesus/ʿĪsā, and Muhammad, who are all identified as both prophets and messengers. At times, it has been suggested that messengers are sent to particular smaller communities of people, while a prophet's audience is broader, but this distinction is not completely supported by the Qur'an. Some scholars have argued that the primary difference between a prophet and a messenger is that the latter brings a book to his people while prophets do not. But this way of distinguishing the two does not hold up in the case of David/Dāwūd because the Qur'an says that God gave him the Psalms, but he is never identified as a messenger in the text (4:163; 17:55).

There is a similar ambiguity with the prophet Abraham/Ibrāhīm, who is never called a messenger in the Qur'an despite the very important role he plays throughout it. Nonetheless, there is some circumstantial evidence to suggest that he might indeed be a messenger. Much of chapter 26 of the Qur'an relates events in the lives of Abraham/Ibrāhīm and six other individuals: Moses/Mūsā, Noah/Nūḥ, Hūd, Ṣāliḥ, Lot/Lūṭ, and Shu'ayb. All seven stories have a common pattern in that they depict these figures urging their people to reject false belief and worship the one God. While the other six are specifically identified as messengers, Abraham/Ibrāhīm is never given that title. Do the similarities between his story and those of the others suggest that he is, in fact, considered to be a messenger in the Qur'an? Strengthening the case that this is so for Abraham/Ibrāhīm, and perhaps others, is the fact that the Qur'an acknowledges that it does not cite all the messengers by name. "We have indeed sent messengers before you (Muhammad), some of which We have told you about and others of which We have not told you about" (40:78a; cf. 4:164). According to one tradition, God sent more than three hundred prophets and well over 120,000 messengers to humanity throughout history.

Muhammad is the quintessential messenger of God in the Qur'an, as these words indicate. "Muhammad is God's messenger. Those who are with him are severe against the unbelievers, and they are compassionate to one another" (48:29; cf. 7:158). The phrase "God and His messenger" is found eighty-five times throughout the Qur'an, and Muhammad is the model that all believers are to emulate. "The messenger of God is indeed an excellent example for you—those who hope in God and the last day, and who remember God often" (33:21). The privileged place that Muhammad enjoys is explained by the idea that some messengers, like some prophets, rank higher than others. "Those are the messengers, some of whom We have favored over others. Among them are some to whom God has spoken, and some whom He has elevated in rank" (2:253a). At the same time, the Qur'an urges people to respect all of the messengers equally. "Those who believe in God and His messengers and who make no distinctions among them—He will reward them. God is the forgiving one, the merciful one" (4:152).

Despite those admonitions, however, the Qur'an recounts that the messengers were often treated harshly by the people to whom they were sent. They were regularly mocked (15:11) and accused of lying (23:44), and some were even put to death (2:87; 5:70). These references to the persecution and pain that came with being a *rasūl* serve an important rhetorical function in the Qur'an because they help to legitimate Muhammad's role as a messenger. The suffering and rejection he experienced did not cast doubt on his status as one sent by God, but actually served to validate it because this was precisely what his prophetic predecessors had to undergo. There is even a verse in the Qur'an that states that Satan/

Shayṭān is an enemy of prophets and messengers, who tries to influence them to go astray (22:52). The entire history of those who came before him demonstrates that to be God's envoy is to be mistreated and misunderstood, and so the passages that describe what the messengers of the past had to endure indirectly confirm Muhammad's standing as one of them.

Questions/Issues

(1) How does the role of the messenger compare to that of the prophet?
(2) What is your reaction to the interpretation that the offices of messenger and prophet are limited to males only?
(3) Do you think that Abraham/Ibrāhīm should be considered to be a messenger in Islam?

Further Reading

Ibrahim, Zakyi. "A Prophet or a Messenger: How Bona Fide a Qur'anic Concept?" *The American Journal of Islamic Social Sciences* 26/1 (2009), 20–46.

35

Messiah/al-Masīḥ

Qur'an 3:45; 4:157; 4:171; 5:75; 5:17, 72; 9:30–31; 4:172

The title "the Messiah/al-Masīḥ" is found eleven times in the Qur'an, always with the definite article, and in every case it is used in reference to Jesus/ʿĪsā. Five times it is followed by the words "Jesus, son of Mary/Maryam," three times it precedes the phrase "son of Mary/Maryam," and the title is found alone in its other three occurrences. While dozens of Arabic etymologies have been proposed for the word, it is most likely a borrowing of the Hebrew term that is used in the Bible to describe a king as the "anointed one," in reference to the ritual that established his authority when he took the throne.

The Qur'an does not provide a description of the role of the Messiah/al-Masīḥ, and, given the fact that the designation is used only for Jesus/ʿĪsā, it is probable that the title was adopted due to Christian usage of it without full understanding of its meaning. It sometimes appears that the Qur'an considers it to be part of Jesus's/ʿĪsā's name, as in its first appearance in the text when angels inform Mary/Maryam that she is pregnant. "Oh Mary, God gives you the good news of a word from Him. His name will be the Messiah Jesus, the son of Mary, who will be eminent in this world and the next, and will be one of those brought near" (3:45).

One verse has the Jews falsely claim that they put the Messiah/al-Masīḥ to death (4:157), but the vast majority of the Qur'an's references to him challenge the Christian belief that he is the son of God. Twice it is stated that the Messiah/al-Masīḥ was nothing more than a messenger (4:171; 5:75), and in two other places the Qur'an teaches that those who say that the Messiah/al-Masīḥ is God are in grave error (5:17, 72). Another verse attributes Christians' false beliefs to their blindly following those from previous generations and simply repeating what they have heard from others (9:30). The next verse goes on to criticize Christians for engaging in *shirk*, the sin of associating something or someone in creation with God and thereby violating the divine unity. "They have taken their leaders and monks and the Messiah, son of Mary, as lords apart from God. They were not commanded anything except to worship the one God. There is no God but He. Praise be to Him above what they associate" (9:31).

The Qur'an asserts that Jesus/`Īsā made no claims of divinity for himself, and that he placed himself in a subservient position to the deity. "The Messiah would not disdain to be God's servant" (4:172). Elsewhere, Jesus/`Īsā refutes the idea that he is equal to God, and he then warns of the punishment that awaits those who continue to maintain that belief. It is the only passage in the Qur'an in which he speaks as the Messiah/al-Masīḥ. "They disbelieve who say, 'God is the Messiah, the son of Mary.' The Messiah said, 'Oh children of Israel, worship God, my Lord and your Lord. Whoever associates something with God, paradise has been denied to that person by God, and the fire will be their abode. There will be no help for the evildoers'" (5:72).

The Qur'an does not associate the Messiah/al-Masīḥ with the line of David/Dāwūd, a connection made in the Bible, nor does it give him the eschatological role at the end time that he plays in Judaism.

Questions/Issues

(1) Are there any other possible reasons why the Qur'an does not define the title "the Messiah/al-Masīḥ"?

36

Michael/Mīkāl

Qur'an 2:98

The Qur'an contains a single reference to the angel Michael/Mīkāl, and it is found in a verse that also mentions Gabriel/Jibrīl. "Whoever is an enemy to God, His angels, His messengers, and Gabriel and Michael—truly, God is an enemy to the disbelievers" (2:98). The arrangement of the sentence in which their names are placed after the word "angels" could suggest that they do not belong in that category, but it is also possible that this is a way of giving Michael/Mīkāl and Gabriel/Jibrīl special status as preeminent within the angelic ranks. In biblical literature, Michael/Mīkāl is depicted as a special guardian of Israel and sometimes serves as a protector or quasi-military leader who fights on God's behalf. He is mentioned only in the book of Daniel in the Hebrew Bible, where he is described as a prince in charge of the people of God (Dan. 10:13, 21; 12:1). In the New Testament he is cited twice, where he is Satan's enemy who overcomes the forces of evil (Jude 9; Rev. 12:7). Michael/Mīkāl is not directly associated with these same qualities in the Qur'an.

37

Moses/Mūsā

Qur'an 19:51–53; 17:2; 20:37–40; 28:3–13; 20:9–36; 26:10–22; 27:7–12; 28:29–35; 20:41–73; 7:103–37; 10:75–89; 26:16–51; 43:47–48; 7:133; 7:148–54; 20:86–98; 28:14–28; 7:134–40; 10:90–92; 20:77–79; 26:52–67; 2:57–61; 5:21–26; 7:142–46

With 115 mentions of his name in the text, Moses/Mūsā is the most frequently cited person in the Qur'an. More attention is devoted to him than to any other biblical figure, and the Qur'an contains many parallels to the Hebrew Bible traditions about Moses/Mūsā. While these stories often have much in common with one another, they are never identical since the details within them sometimes vary considerably. In addition, on occasion the Qur'an contains multiple versions of some stories that are recounted only one time in the Bible. The material related to Moses/Mūsā in the Qur'an is spread out across more than thirty chapters, and the longest section that tells his story is nearly ninety verses in length (20:9–97). The extensive amount of coverage Moses/Mūsā receives in the Qur'an makes a comprehensive treatment impossible, so the discussion here will be limited to a number of scenes that are familiar to many Bible readers.

A brief summary of Moses's/Mūsā's role in the Qur'an is provided in this verse. "Remember Moses in the book. Truly, he was a chosen one, a messenger, and a prophet. We called him from the right side of the mount and drew him near in communion. We gave him, out of Our mercy, his brother Aaron, a prophet." (19:51–53). This passage specifically identifies Moses/Mūsā as a prophetic messenger, and it conforms well to the Bible's portrayal of him. In particular, the mention of "the mount" recalls the key role that Mount Sinai plays as the location where God gives the law to Moses/Mūsā (Exod. 19). In the same way, the idea that he and God communed privately is a recurring biblical theme as Moses/Mūsā has frequent intimate encounters with the deity during which the divine will is revealed to him (Exod. 33:11). In the same way, the reference to Aaron/Hārūn echoes his brother's function in the Hebrew Bible, where he is often depicted as Moses's/Mūsā's partner and helper (Exod. 4:10–17). One important aspect of Moses's/Mūsā's identity in the Qur'an that is only hinted at in this passage, with its designation of him as a messenger, is his role as the recipient of a book given to him by God. "We gave Moses the book, and We made it a guidance for the people of Israel so that they would not take a protector apart from Me" (17:2). Moses/Mūsā, like Jesus/`Īsā and Muhammad after him, was one of the prophets who were entrusted with a written text meant to be authoritative for his community, and the Qur'an identifies that book as the Torah.

The birth story of Moses/Mūsā is recounted twice in the Qur'an. It is briefly alluded to in one version of the burning bush episode, when God reminds Moses/Mūsā that his mother had followed the deity's instructions to put the child in a basket and float him on the river so he would not be harmed, and that he was eventually restored to his mother with his sister's assistance (20:37–40). The other passage, found in 28:3–13, is a lengthier account that describes the events in more detail and is both similar to and different from the biblical story in Exodus 2:1–10. The similarities include the Egyptian setting, a Pharaoh/Fir`awn who is ruthless, the child's deliverance via the river, the rescue of Moses/Mūsā by someone in Pharaoh's/Fir`awn's family, and the child's return to his mother with the help of his sister. The key differences in the Qur'an's version are the following: (1) there is no explicit mention of the child being put in a basket; (2) it is Pharaoh's/Fir`awn's wife, rather than his daughter as in the Bible, who brings the child into the Egyptian ruler's household; (3) his mother does not return Moses/Mūsā after she has finished nursing him; and (4) a member of Pharaoh's/Fir`awn's court named Haman/Hāmān plays a role in the story.

The most profound difference in the way the Bible and the Qur'an relate the story of Moses's/Mūsā's birth is the critical role that God plays throughout the latter text. His mother floats the child on the river because the deity commands her to do so (v.7). When it appears that she is wavering and about to admit what she has done, God strengthens the mother's heart (v.10). The deity exercises control over the baby's feeding habits so that he refuses to nurse (v.12). God is the one responsible for returning Moses/Mūsā to his mother and reuniting the two (v.13). As the plot unfolds, it is clear that God is responsible for what takes place each step of the way. This is in sharp contrast to the biblical account, where the deity is not mentioned a single time, and it is an example of how the story has been Islamized. The Qur'an teaches that God is responsible for all things, and this idea is reflected in the way the text conveys the events surrounding the birth of Moses/Mūsā. The Islamization of the tradition can also be seen in verse 7 when God assures his mother that Moses/Mūsā will be a messenger, a title that has heavy theological significance in the Qur'an and Islam.

The Qur'an recounts the story of Moses/Mūsā at the burning bush, during which God instructs him to go to Pharaoh/Fira`awn and urge him to set free the Israelite people. This episode is found in several passages of the text, some of which do not mention the fire specifically, and here the focus will be on the version in 20:9–36 (cf. 26:10–22; 27:7–12; 28:29–35). Both this passage and the biblical account in Exodus 3:1–4:17 describe a conversation between God and Moses/Mūsā, but the ways they do so vary somewhat. In the first place, the biblical description of the encounter is nearly four times longer than what is found in the Qur'an. This discrepancy in length is mainly due to the fact that Moses/Mūsā is much more reluctant to obey God's command in Exodus than he is in the Islamic text, and so the deity has to do more in the Bible to convince him to go to Pharaoh/Fir`awn. There are seven exchanges between God and Moses/Mūsā in Exodus, and the latter comes up with one excuse after another to avoid paying a visit to the Egyptian ruler. The Qur'an lacks this hesitancy on Moses's/Mūsā's part, and it does not report multiple exchanges between the two, as God speaks first and then Moses/Mūsā responds. While Moses/Mūsā is repeatedly told to go to Pharaoh/Fir`awn in Exodus, this commission comes only at the end of God's words in the Qur'an (v.24).

Moses's/Mūsā's response to God has a completely different tone in the Qur'an. In the Bible, he interrupts the deity frequently and he uses every avoidance strategy at his disposal to get around having to visit Pharaoh/Fir`awn, including averting his eyes, questioning God's authority, using self-deprecating language, and raising hypothetical scenarios. In the Qur'an, Moses/Mūsā waits until God is finished before he begins to speak, and he seeks the deity's assistance to carry out his charge. In Exodus, Moses/Mūsā rebels against God's will, but in the Qur'an he depends on God and seeks divine aid. This can be seen in how the two texts describe Moses's/Mūsā's acknowledgment that he is a poor speaker. In the Bible, he uses this as an excuse to be relieved of the burden of going to the Egyptian leader because he will not be able to effectively communicate with him (Exod. 4:10), but in the Qur'an Moses/Mūsā asks for God's help to improve his ability to speak with Pharaoh/Fir`awn (vv.27–28). The result is a completely different portrait of Moses/Mūsā in the two texts—the resistant protestor of the Bible has been replaced with a receptive partner in the Qur'an.

Similar to the burning bush episode, the Qur'an contains multiple accounts of the plagues story that is narrated in Exodus 7–11 during which Moses/Mūsā and Aaron/Hārūn send divine punishments on Pharaoh/Fir`awn and his people in order to convince the ruler to let the Israelites leave Egypt. The passage that will be discussed here is found in 20:41–73, but the events are also recounted in 7:103–37, 10:75–89, and 26:16–51. This text does not refer directly to plagues, but it twice mentions signs from God (vv.42, 56). Elsewhere the Qur'an makes a direct link between the signs and the plagues. The punishing nature of the signs is stressed in their ascending levels of harshness, "When he came to them with Our signs, they laughed at them. Each sign We showed them was greater than its (preceding) sister, and We seized them with punishment so that they might return" (43:47–48). Another verse makes a direct correlation between some of the plagues of the book of Exodus and the signs of the Qur'an. "We sent to them the storm, the locusts, the lice, the frogs, and the blood—clear signs. But they were proud and sinful people" (7:133).

Aaron/Hārūn has a more prominent role in the biblical story than he does in the Qur'an, where Moses/Mūsā is the dominant figure and Aaron/Hārūn does not speak or act on his own. Their charge in the Qur'an is to "speak gently" to the Egyptian ruler (v.44), and Pharaoh's/Fir`awn's fate rests more on what the two brothers say than on what they do. The Qur'an story does not mention God's hardening of Pharaoh's/Fir`awn's heart, which is a central theme throughout the biblical account. Moses/Mūsā and Aaron/Hārūn have a conversation with Pharaoh/Fir`awn in an effort to teach him about God (vv.49–52), and it is only after he refuses to accept their words that the signs are sent (v.56).

The focus in the Qur'an is not on the signs themselves, but on how people respond to them. This is illustrated in how Pharaoh's/Fir`awn's magicians are presented in the text. In both the Bible and the Qur'an they acknowledge the authority of Moses's/Mūsā's God, but they come to that realization differently in the two texts. It is a longer process in the biblical story, where they have multiple contests with Moses/Mūsā and his brother before they recognize God's power. In the Qur'an there is a single contest that is similar to the one involving the staffs that turn into snakes that is mentioned in Exodus (7:8–13), and their response of faith is immediate and more explicit than it is in the Bible. "The magicians fell down prostrate saying, 'We believe in the Lord of Aaron and Moses!' " (v.70; cf. Exod. 8:18–19). After Pharaoh/Fir`awn tries to win them back by threatening them, they reject him outright and express their allegiance to the God of Moses/ Mūsā. "Truly, we believe in our Lord so that He might forgive our sins and the magic you forced us to practice. God is the best and most lasting" (v.73). The last mention of the magicians in the Bible describes how they suffered from the boils that were afflicting everyone else in Egypt (Exod. 9:11), but in the Qur'an those external marks have been replaced with the internal mark of faith.

The theme of the hardening of Pharaoh's/Fir`awn's heart makes him a somewhat sympathetic figure in Exodus. Several times he wishes to do the right thing and let the Israelites go, but each time he is prevented from doing so because God has hardened his heart (Exod. 9:27–35; 10:16–20). In the Qur'an this element is missing, as God instructs Moses/Mūsā to go and speak to the Egyptian leader in the hope that his heart will be softened. "Speak to him gently. Perhaps he will remember or fear" (v.44). Unlike in Exodus, where God is the one who is responsible for his hardened heart, the Pharaoh/Fir`awn of the Qur'an can blame no one but himself for his refusal to heed Moses's/Mūsā's request. In this way, the story becomes one of human response and personal responsibility, rather than one of divine might and control. The Pharaoh/Fir`awn of Exodus has no choice, but his counterpart in the Qur'an makes the wrong choice. This aspect of his character in the Qur'an is captured well through the use of repetition. In this verse God tells Moses/Mūsā to inform the Egyptian monarch that, "Truly, it has been revealed to us that punishment will be upon the one who rejects and *turns away*" (v.48) The last verb in that sentence appears a bit later in the passage to reveal Pharaoh/Fir`awn as the guilty party. "So Pharaoh *turned away* to draw up his strategy, and then he returned" (v.60).

The Qur'an contains two versions of the golden calf story that is recounted in the Bible in Exodus 32. The one that will be examined here is found in 7:148–54, while the other is at 20:86–98. As in the Moses/Mūsā traditions explored above, the overall plot of the Qur'an narrative mirrors that of the Bible, but there are fairly significant differences in the details of the two. Once again, a consideration of how each character or set of characters is presented will help to make those differences apparent.

The Israelites say very little in either text, but the few words they speak in both are revealing. They have two lines of dialogue in the Bible, and each is uttered while Moses/Mūsā is still up on the mountain communing with God. In both of their statements they demonstrate that they have forgotten that it was God who brought them out of Egypt (Exod. 32:1, 4). In the chapter's first verse they claim that it was Moses/Mūsā who rescued them, and the second time they speak they say that it was the work of the gods represented by the golden calf. At no time do they express regret for what they have done, and the text clearly criticizes the people for their actions (Exod. 32: 6, 25). In contrast, the Israelites speak only one time in the Qur'an passage and their words convey a sense of remorse that they lack in Exodus. "When they repented and realized that they had gone astray they said, 'If our Lord will not have mercy on us and forgive us our sins, we will surely be among the lost ones'" (v.149).

Aaron/Hārūn is not mentioned by name in the Qur'an, where he is referred to as Moses's/Mūsā's brother. His only appearance in the story takes place when Moses/Mūsā returns from the mountain and angrily grabs Aaron/Hārūn by his hair, causing him to proclaim his innocence by stating that the people wanted to kill him (v.150). The biblical story gives Aaron/Hārūn a more prominent role by describing how he fashioned the calf in a mold that he had prepared, built an altar for it, and then called for a feast (Exod. 32:2–6). In addition, it blames him for his laxity and culpability (Exod. 32:25, 35). Therefore he comes across as disingenuous and deceptive when he protests that he is innocent of any wrong-doing when Moses/Mūsā confronts him (Exod. 42:21–24). In the Qur'an, on the other hand, his assertion that he is blameless has a ring of truth to it because the text plainly states that it was the Israelites, and not Aaron/Hārūn, who built the calf (v.148).

The character of Moses/Mūsā undergoes a transformation in both texts, but the change is markedly different in each. In the biblical story he initially defends the people as he persuades God not to destroy them for their offense (Exod. 32:7–14). But once he leaves the mountain and returns to them, he gets progressively angrier with the Israelites. First, he smashes the tablets, an action that symbolizes the fracturing of the covenantal relationship between God and the people (Exod. 32:19). He then burns the calf, grinds it to powder that is mixed in water, and forces the Israelites to drink it (Exod. 32:20). His final reaction is the most violent as the Levites obey his command to "kill your brother, your friend, your neighbor," which results in the deaths of 3,000 people (Exod. 32:25–29). This is quite a change from the Moses/Mūsā on the mountain just a few verses earlier, who spoke up on behalf of the Israelites when God was prepared to annihilate them.

In the Qur'an, things move in the opposite direction. When he returns from his encounter with God, Moses/Mūsā angrily lashes out at the people and accuses them of bringing divine judgment on themselves. He then turns on his brother and pulls him by the hair (v.150), but there is a noticeable shift in his demeanor once Aaron/Hārūn responds. No longer irate, Moses/Mūsā appeals to God and begs forgiveness for himself and his brother (v.151). The people are not included in his prayer because they have already acknowledged their sin and repented, but Moses/Mūsā realizes that he and Aaron/Hārūn have failed in their duty as prophets to keep the Israelites on the straight path and so he asks for God's mercy on the two of them. The Qur'an also reports that Moses/Mūsā had thrown down the tablets when he descended the mountain, but they do not break as they do in Exodus because he is able to retrieve them after his prayer.

The last reference to Moses/Mūsā in the Qur'an story highlights his transformation from enraged to tranquil and explains that the relationships among the characters have been restored. "When Moses' anger had subsided, he took the tablets. In their writing is guidance and mercy for those who fear their Lord" (v.154).

In the biblical story, the divine character is associated with death and destruction. Moses/Mūsā is able to convince God to not punish the Israelites, but the deity's rage still simmers and is expressed as the story unfolds. The order from Moses/Mūsā to kill fellow Israelites that the Levites follow is actually a command that comes from God (Exod. 32:27), but even the 3,000 deaths that ensue are not enough to satisfy the divine desire for punishment because the chapter ends with a reference to a plague that God sends on the people (Exod. 32:35). In the Qur'an, however, the deity is associated with peace and forgiveness as every character in the story comes to experience God's mercy. This aspect of the divine/human relationship is summed up well in these verses, which lay out the two options that each person must choose from. "Anger from their Lord and humiliation in the present life will come to those who took the calf. Thus do We repay those who invent falsehood. But for those who do evil and then repent and believe, truly your Lord is forgiving and merciful after that" (vv. 152–53). The Qur'an's version of the golden calf story describes the rewards that the Israelites, Aaron/Hārūn, and Moses/Mūsā experienced because they chose the latter option.

Among the other traditions in the Qur'an about Moses/Mūsā and the Israelites that have parallels in the biblical literature are the following: his killing of a man while in Egypt that causes him to flee (28:14–28; cf. Exod. 2:11–22); the Exodus story in which he leads the Israelites out of Egypt (7:134–40; 10:90–92; 20:77–79; 26:52–67; cf. Exod. 14); events associated with the wandering in the wilderness (2:57–61; 5:21–26; cf. Exod. 16:4–36; Num. 13–14); and Moses's/Mūsā's meeting with God on a mountain (7:142–46; cf. Exod. 33:18–23).

"The Stories of the Prophets" literature relates a number of traditions about Moses's/Mūsā's early years that are not in the Qur'an. Moses/Mūsā was miraculously conceived in the house of Pharaoh/Fir`awn, and when he was brought home he escaped detection by being hidden in a hot oven that did not harm him. It is also reported that Moses's/Mūsā's mother placed him in a basket before putting him in the river, Pharaoh/Fir`awn killed young Israelites only in alternate years and that Moses/Mūsā was born in a year in which killings were committed. In many of the traditions about the young Moses/Mūsā in these sources he is already demonstrating and expressing his faith in God and he is the enemy of Pharaoh/Fir`awn.

Moses's/Mūsā's faith during his journey to Midian is stressed by explaining how his only companion on the trip was God and his only provision was piety. The sources further report that during the ten years he lived in Midian Moses/Mūsā found faith in the one God. His wife Zipporah gave birth to their child the same night that Moses/Mūsā had the encounter with God at the burning bush, and she then returned to her father while Moses/Mūsā went to meet with Pharaoh/Firʿawn. The plagues narrative in "The Stories of the Prophets" is fairly lengthy, and they include the details that Aaron/Hārūn worked in the Egyptian court and that Pharaoh/Firʿawn killed his wife for siding with Moses/Mūsā. Like the Qur'an, "The Stories of the Prophets" do not mention the killing of the first-born children of the Egyptians that is found in the biblical account. Some sources contain a lengthy section describing Pharaoh's/Firʿawn's struggles with Moses's/Mūsā's success and his desire to kill him, which is also mentioned in the Qur'an (40:26–45). In addition, they sometimes provide some background information on two other stories involving Moses/Mūsā in the Qur'an—the episode that discusses a cow that the Israelites slaughtered (2:67–74), and his encounter with a mysterious wise figure known as al-Khidr (18:60–82) (al-Kisāʾī; Ibn Kathīr).

Questions/Issues

(1) What are some of the most significant differences in how the Islamic sources and the Bible present Moses/Mūsā?
(2) Do you note any consistent themes in the way the Qur'an describes the four scenes from Moses's/Mūsā's life that are discussed in some detail above?
(3) Choose one of the other traditions involving Moses/Mūsā that are mentioned above and compare how the Bible and the Qur'an describes it.

Further Reading

Wheeler, Brannon M. *Moses in the Qur'an and Islamic Exegesis* (New York: Routledge, 2002).

38

Moses's/Mūsā's Mother

Qur'an 20:37–40; 28:3–14

The mother of Moses/Mūsā is mentioned in both of the Qur'an's accounts that describe his birth and how he was saved from Pharaoh's/Fir`awn's plot to have all the Hebrew newborn boys put to death. The first one is part of the burning bush scene during which God commissions Moses/Mūsā and Aaron/Hārūn to go to the Egyptian ruler and urge him to let their people go. In the course of their conversation, God reminds Moses/Mūsā about how he had earlier received divine favor soon after his birth, when the deity instructed his mother to put him in a basket and float it on the water so the child would escape harm (20:37–40). In this passage Pharaoh/Fir`awn is not referred to specifically, and is simply described as an enemy to both God and Moses/Mūsā (v.39). With the help of his sister, Moses/Mūsā is restored to his mother so she would be at peace and not be sorrowful (v.40).

The mother plays an expanded role in the second version of the story, resulting in a more rounded character with discernible traits (28:3–14). Pharaoh/Fir`awn is referred to directly, and this account opens up with a description of his cruelty toward the Hebrews and God's desire to come to their assistance (vv.3–6). This story does not mention a basket, and so a literal reading of the scene would have the mother put the child directly into the water with no protection at all. God's initial words to her, in which she is ordered to do two contradictory things, express the extreme nature of the deity's command to her. "Suckle him, and if you fear for him toss him into the sea. Do not fear or grieve, for We will restore him to you and make him one of the messengers" (v.7). While the Egyptian location of the story has led commentators to conclude that the baby was placed in the Nile River, the Arabic term in both accounts that describes where she is to place Moses/Mūsā (*yamm*) is normally used for a larger body of water. Despite the danger that she is exposing her child to, the mother is asked to trust in God and to believe that the promise that her son will be restored to her will come to pass.

Once Moses/Mūsā has been sent on his way in the second story, God is not yet done with his mother. "Moses's mother became anxious, and she was about to reveal it had We not strengthened her heart in order that she might be a believer" (v.11). In her moment of weakness, God comes to the assistance of the mother in order to strengthen her faith and to ensure the child's safety. This causes her to ask Moses's/Mūsā's sister to follow the baby to determine where he ends up, and this sets the stage for his eventual return to his mother. The purpose of the reunion of the two is stated in almost identical terms in the two versions, but there is a telling addition in the second one. Both agree that Moses/Mūsā is given back to his mother so she might have joy and not grieve, but the second one also states that they were reunited "in order that she might know that God's promise is true" (v.13). This shifts the focus to Moses's/Mūsā's mother and, unlike in the first passage, one of the main themes of this one is the faith that she has in God and her trust in the divine plan.

The biblical parallel to this story is in Exodus 2:1–10, which shares much in common with the Qur'an's accounts. The most notable difference between the two, which becomes immediately obvious when they are compared to one another, is the complete lack of any reference to God in the biblical passage.

Building on the Qur'anic narrative, "The Stories of the Prophets" and exegetical literature highlight how the mother became afraid after giving birth to Moses/Mūsā, since she had seen thousands of other boys slaughtered. Following God's command, she made a casket, put Moses/Mūsā within it, and placed it in the Nile. The scholars give different accounts of how long Moses/Mūsā was in the river, from three to forty days. Eventually, the child floated to the palace, which was the most guarded place in the land (al-Nadawī).When the people in the palace saw the child, they immediately adored him, played with him, and kissed him. The wife of Pharaoh/Fir`awn, the queen, became especially fond of him and began to love him a great deal. When Pharaoh/Fir`awn saw this he became upset and asked, "What is this?" and he ordered the child to be slaughtered. However, the wife requested that they keep the child and stated, "Here is a joy to behold for me and for you!" (28:9). Pharaoh/Fir`awn replied, "For you, yes. But for me, no! I have no need for him!" (Ibn Kathīr)

"The Stories of the Prophets" go on to report that the child would not suckle with anyone, consistently refusing nourishment and crying. The sister of Moses/Mūsā inquired about her brother at the palace, and the people informed her that there was a child there but that he would not eat. The girl said that she knew a woman who would be able to breast-feed the boy, but at first they did not believe her. In desperation, they agreed to this arrangement and the child was sent with the girl and some servants. When the mother of Moses/Mūsā saw her child, she embraced him and he immediately began to suckle. Pharaoh/Fir`awn became suspicious and asked, "Why did this child accept this woman. Is she his mother?" The mother responded, "Oh sir, I am a woman who has a pleasant scent and good milk, so every child accepts me" (al-Nadawī). Pharaoh/Fir`awn believed her and he provided her a salary for breast-feeding the child. Thus, God returned Moses/Mūsā back to his mother because of her patience and trust in Him.

Some Muslim scholars contend that Moses's/Mūsā's mother was a prophet because the Qur'an uses the Arabic word for revelation (*waḥī*) to describe how God commanded her to throw her son into the sea (Ibn Ḥazm). However, others have rejected that notion by stating that the verb should be understood as referring to inspiration since it is used elsewhere in the Qur'an (16:68) to describe how God communicates with the bees to make honey (al-Rāzī and Ibn Kathīr). Nevertheless, even though the majority of Muslim scholars held that all the prophets were male, the debate demonstrates that some were open to the idea of female prophecy.

Questions/Issues

(1) How does the Qur'an's emphasis on God's relationship with Moses's/Mūsā's mother in 28:3–14 have an effect on how the story is interpreted?
(2) Does the lack of attention on that aspect of the story in 20:37–40 have an impact on its meaning?
(3) How might the complete absence of God in the biblical story of Moses's/Mūsā's birth be explained?
(4) What do you think of the idea of the mother of Moses/Mūsā being a prophet?

Further Reading

Fierro, Maribel. "Women as Prophets in Islam," in *Writing the Feminine: Women in Arab Sources*, ed. Manuela Marin and Randi Deguilhem (London/New York: I. B. Tauris, 2002), 183–98.

Turki, Abdel Magid. "Femmes privilégiées et privilèges féminins dans le système théologique et juridique d'Ibn Ḥazm," *Studia Islamica* 47, (1978): 25–82.

39

Noah/Nūḥ

Qur'an 71:1–28;7:59–64; 10:71–73; 11:25–49; 23:23–30; 26:105–20

Noah/Nūḥ is mentioned more than forty times in the Qur'an in twenty-six chapters. He plays an important role in the text as a prophet of warning, who is sent to convince his people to reject polytheism and follow the one true God. The most detailed account of his message is given in chapter 71, which has the name "Nūḥ" and is entirely devoted to his prophetic career. In his opening words he identifies himself as a "clear warner" to his people (71:2), and he urges them to serve God in order to have their sins forgiven and be saved (71:4). He then addresses the deity as he explains that his call to ask for mercy and to acknowledge God as the one responsible for all that exists has been ignored (71:5–24). This leads to the drowning of the unbelievers and their banishment to hell (71:25).

The Qur'an contains several accounts of the flood story, although the deluge itself is not described in any detail (7:59–64; 10:71–73; 11:25–49; 23:23–30; 26:105–20). In each case, Noah/Nūḥ is sent to his people and he delivers his message of warning, but they mock him and refuse to heed his words. He and a few others are saved by riding out the flood on a ship, while the rest are drowned. The length of time the flood lasted for and its geographical extent are not mentioned in the Qur'an. The passage in chapter 11 is the longest version of the flood story, and it contains some elements not found in the other accounts. Its first half describes events that occur prior to the flood, and the second half recounts the building of the ark, the inundation itself, and what takes place after the floodwaters subside. The close connection between Noah/Nūḥ and his audience is highlighted by the way he addresses them as "My people!" at the beginning of three consecutive verses as he urges them to mend their ways (11:28–30). In addition, they are referred to as "his" or "your" people four other times in the text prior to the flood. In the Qur'an, Noah/Nūḥ is a man of many words. He is the subject of ten verbs in the passage, and all but one (11:38, when he builds the ark) relate to the act of speaking.

Human sin is personified and exemplified in Noah's/Nūḥ's detractors, who reject him in a stinging series of three statements. "We see you as nothing but a human being like ourselves. We see that the only ones who follow you seem to be the most despised among us. We do not see you as better than we are, and we think you are liars" (11:27). Their triple use of the verb "to see" indicates that his people's error is one of perspective as they are incapable of perceiving things as they really are. Noah/Nūḥ responds in kind by calling attention to their lack of sight—"My people! Do you not see?" (11:28). The presence of a rare anthropomorphism in reference to God a little later in the story might be a subtle wordplay meant to call attention to where true sight resides. "Build the ark under Our eyes and Our inspiration" (11:37a). As is the case in other punishment stories in the Qur'an, the flood is caused by people's rejection of a prophet sent by God because of their inability to recognize his authority.

The people saved from the flood include most members of Noah's/Nūḥ's family and those others who have believed his message. "When Our command came and the fountains gushed forth, We said, 'Load on it (the ark) a pair of every kind and your family, except for the one against whom the word has already gone forth, and whoever believes.' But only a few believed with him" (11:40). The Qur'an does not specify how many believers not in Noah's/Nūḥ's family were spared. It is implied that the members of his family who survived were believers, and this is confirmed in the tragic story of the one member who is drowned in the flood. Noah's/Nūḥ's son's fate is foreshadowed in verse 40 with its reference to "the one against whom the word has already gone forth," and his demise comes to pass a few verses later when he refuses to heed his father's advice.

> Noah cried out to his son who was standing apart, "Oh son, get on with us and do not be with the unbelievers." He said, "I will take refuge to a mountain that will protect me from the water." He (Noah) said, "There is no protection today from the decree of God except for the one to whom He shows mercy." And a wave came between them, and he was among the drowned. (11:42b-43)

In this episode that highlights human free will, Noah's/Nūḥ's son represents unbelievers who cling to their false gods, and it points out that even a prophet's own offspring can make the wrong choice and is not guaranteed salvation simply on the basis of lineage. This is a lesson Noah/Nūḥ is reminded of when he goes on to question the deity about his son's death and cries out, "Lord, my son is of my family! Surely Your promise is true, and You are the most just of judges"

(11:45). God's response indicates that a new understanding of family is being put forward, one that is based on belief rather than biology. "He said, 'Oh Noah, he is not of your family for he is an unrighteous work. Do not ask Me about that of which you have no knowledge. I admonish you to not be one of the ignorant ones" (11:46). This leads Noah/Nūḥ to ask God for mercy and forgiveness. The deity does not punish Noah/Nūḥ, but puts him in his place nonetheless. The prophet is forced to practice what he has been preaching and accept the divine will, even if it means the loss of his son. The distinction between the faithful father and the unfaithful son highlights the two options before each person.

Because his people have been cautioned by Noah/Nūḥ, the flood does not come upon them out of the blue. In a sense, his contemporaries force God's hand by challenging Noah/Nūḥ to follow through on his warnings to them. "They said, 'Oh Noah, you have argued with us long and hard. Bring on us what you threaten us with, if you are among the truthful'" (11:32). Despite the punishment they receive, the main quality of the deity stressed in the passage is mercy, something Noah/Nūḥ alludes to four times (11:28, 41, 43, 47). In 11:47 Noah/Nūḥ seeks divine forgiveness for himself just as Adam/Ādam and Eve/Ḥawwā' do, after they eat of the tree of the garden that has been forbidden to them. "He said, 'Lord, I seek Your protection for asking You about what I have no knowledge. Unless You forgive me and show me mercy, I will be among the lost ones" (7:23).

The Prophet Muhammad is addressed in a verse, which is an apparent reference to his own people's inability to accept the message he brought to them. "Do they say, 'He has fabricated it.'? Say (Muhammad), 'If I have fabricated it may my guilt be upon me, but I am innocent of the crimes you commit'" (11:35). The passage ends with a similar comment directed to Muhammad. "This is part of the tidings we reveal to you (Muhammad). You did not know it before this, nor did your people. Be patient, for the end is for the pious" (11:49). In this way, the story of Noah/Nūḥ and the flood, like many of the traditions about the prior prophets, functions as an interpretive lens for Muhammad, his audience, and later readers that attempts to legitimate his prophetic career. The consistent prophetic paradigm throughout the Qur'an is one in which the prophet is called by God to deliver a message to his people, is rejected by them, but is eventually vindicated by the deity. The fact that Muhammad has undergone the same experiences as Noah/Nūḥ and the other prophets of the past is an indication that he is among their ranks.

"The Stories of the Prophets" literature includes interesting details in the story regarding how Noah/Nūḥ was mocked by his people, the description of the ark, and the immensity of the flood. The literature explains how the ark was constructed and states that it took years to make. Noah/Nūḥ planted trees for twenty years, and he stopped preaching to his people during this time. As he cut down the trees and began to construct the ark, his people began to make fun of him by taunting "the prophet has now become a carpenter" (al-Ṭarafī).

Drawing from biblical narratives, "The Stories of the Prophets" debate how immense the ark was, with some stating it was 300 arm lengths long and 50 wide. Others claim that it was even larger, with al-Kisāʾī specifying that it was 1,000 arm lengths long and 500 wide. When the ark was completed, Noah/Nūḥ began to herd a pair—male and female—of each type of animal into it. Noah/Nūḥ put all of its occupants on different levels of the ark, with one level for the animals, another for human beings, and a third for the birds (al-Ṭarafī). Others sources mention that Noah/Nūḥ put the carnivores on a different level so they would not eat the livestock. A sizable number of people also entered the ark, with the numbers ranging from ten to eighty.

Debates also circle around whether the wife of Noah/Nūḥ, who is mentioned in the Qur'an as one of the disbelievers, entered the ark. Most commentators believe that she perished in the flood in response to Noah's/Nūḥ's Qur'anic prayer that God destroy all the disbelievers. The literature also emphasizes the immensity of the flood and the precarious nature of the journey. The waves were eighty arm lengths tall and the flood encompassed the entire world, leaving no living thing spared. The journey lasted a total of 150 days, and it covered a tremendous distance (Ibn Kathīr). Some commentators also note that God took the ark on a tour of various religious sites. As they passed by Jerusalem a voice cried, "Oh Noah/Nūḥ, this is Jerusalem where the prophets of your children will live." Then the waves took the boat to Mecca, where it circumambulated the Kaʿba seven times, similar to how Muslims perform the ritual during the Islamic pilgrimage (al-Kisāʾī).

When the rain ended, Noah/Nūḥ sent a raven out to examine the earth but it did not return to him. He then sent out a dove which flew from the east to the west. It then returned to Noah/Nūḥ after he called for it and it said, "Oh prophet of God, the earth has been destroyed and everyone on it. As for the water, I do not see it except in the land of India and there is no tree left on the face of the earth except an olive tree and it is [still] green, it did not change [during the flood]." Then God revealed, "Oh Noah/Nūḥ, descend in peace from Us, with blessings on you and on some of the communities that will spring from those who are with you" (11:48). The inhabitants of the ark then descended on to the earth and God returned the day and night as they were, as well as the stars, plants, and trees (al- Kisā'ī). In these ways, "The Stories of the Prophets" literature emphasizes how Noah/Nūḥ was mocked for his belief in God, the immensity of the ark, the deluge that covered the entire earth, and humanity's return back to land.

Questions/Issues

(1) How does the biblical flood story (Gen. 6–9) compare to the one in the Qur'an?
(2) What impact do Noah's/Nūḥ's speeches in the Islamic sources have on the reader's interpretation of the story?
(3) What lessons can be drawn from the episode involving Noah's/Nūḥ's son?

Further Reading

Lodahl, Michael. *Claiming Abraham: Reading the Bible and the Qur'an Side by Side* (Grand Rapids: Brazos Press, 2010), pp.113–26.

Wheeler, Brannon M. *Prophets in the Quran: An Introduction to the Quran and Muslim Exegesis* (London: Continuum, 2002), pp. 49–62.

40

Pharaoh/Fir`awn

Qur'an 7:127, 141; 14:6; 28:1–14; 10:83; 20:24, 41–73; 10:88; 79:15–26; 26:23–51; 11:96–99; 7:123–24; 2:49–50; 8:52–54; 17:101–4; 20:77–79; 28:36–42; 43:46–56; 51:38–40; 10:90–92

The ruler of Egypt known as Pharaoh in the Bible is identified as Fir`awn in the Qur'an, where he is mentioned almost seventy-five times. In the Islamic text the word never takes the definite article as "the Pharaoh/Fir`awn." It is therefore unclear if it should be understood to be a title as it is in the Bible and the ancient Egyptian language, where its literal meaning is "the Great House" in reference to the royal residence. The Qur'an's lengthiest narrative involving the Egyptian ruler is the story of Joseph/Yūsuf that takes up the entirety of chapter 12, but there he is consistently referred to as "king" (*malik*) and not "Pharaoh/Fir`awn."

Virtually all of the allusions to Pharaoh/Fir`awn in the Qur'an are in the context of traditions about how Moses/Mūsā liberated the Israelites from the tyranny of the Egyptian monarch. Similar to the biblical account, his decree calling for the death of all Israelite male children is what causes Moses's/Mūsā's mother to place her child in the river where he is rescued by a member of Pharaoh's/Fir`awn's family (7:127, 141; 14:6; 28:1–14). Pharaoh/Fir`awn is consistently presented in negative terms in the Qur'an as a ruthless oppressor who transgressed the bounds of decency and justice (10:83; 20:24, 43). When Moses/Mūsā and Aaron/Hārūn attempt to persuade him to release the Israelites through their display of signs and plagues from God, Pharaoh/Fir`awn stubbornly refuses to do so (20:41–73). In the biblical story, God's hardening of Pharaoh's/Fir`awn's heart is the main reason why the Egyptian does not agree to the demands of Moses/Mūsā and Aaron/Hārūn, but this is not a dominant motif in the Qur'an (the lone mention of it is in 10:88). Human free will, not divine influence over Pharaoh's/Fir`awn's actions, is to the fore in the Qur'an. As his words to Moses/Mūsā make clear, God wants the Egyptian leader's heart to be softened rather than hardened. "Speak to him gently. Perhaps he will remember or fear" (20:44).

Despite Moses's/Mūsā's best efforts, Pharaoh/Fir`awn remains unmoved as he holds fast to his belief that he is the highest Lord (79:15–26) and ascribes divinity to himself (26:23–51). The end result is that he will be the ruin of his own people, who will follow him into hell (11:96–99). Those who refuse to obey him are threatened with unspeakable torture, especially if they come to have faith in the God of Moses/Mūsā. "He said, 'Do you believe in him before I give you permission? He must be your chief who taught you magic. I will surely cut off your hands and feet on alternate sides and crucify you on trunks of palm trees. You will come to know which of us has a harsher and more lasting punishment!" (20:71; cf. 7:123–24; 26:49).

The Israelites eventually were able to flee from the clutches of Pharaoh/Fir`awn and escape Egypt by miraculously passing through a body of water in a way similar to what is described in Exodus 14. The Bible does not state explicitly that Pharaoh/Fir`awn was drowned along with his forces, but that is the case in the Qur'an (2:49–50; 8:52–54; 17:101–4; 20:77–79; 28:36–42; 43:46–56; 51:38–40). One passage presents an alternative account of the fate of Pharaoh/Fir`awn that describes a remarkable conversion on his part as he confronts his mortality. Commentators debate whether or not Pharaoh/Fir`awn survived his watery ordeal, but there is no doubt that this is a dramatic example of the theme of God's mercy that is at the heart of the Qur'an's message.

> We brought the children of Israel across the sea and Pharaoh and his troops followed them wickedly and maliciously until, as he was about to drown, he cried out, "I believe that there is no god but the one the children of Israel believe in, and I am among those who submit." What? Prior to this you were rebellious and one of the corrupt. Today, We will save you bodily so that you may be a sign for those who come after you. Truly, many people do not heed Our signs. (10:90–92)

Questions/Issues

(1) How does the downplaying of the hardening of Pharaoh's/Fir`awn's heart affect how he is presented in the Qur'an compared to the Bible?

(2) Does the Qur'an tradition about Pharaoh/Fir`awn coming to believe in the God of Moses/Mūsā rehabilitate his image in the Qur'an?

(3) Does Pharaoh/Fir`awn come across as more of a villain in the Bible or the Qur'an?

Further Reading

Tottoli, Roberto. *Biblical Prophets in the Qur'an and Muslim Literature* (London: Routledge, 2002), pp.31–35.

41

Pharaoh's/Fir`awn's Family

Qur'an 28:3–14

In both the Bible and the Qur'an a member of Pharaoh's/Fir`awn's family plays a role in rescuing the infant Moses/Mūsā after his mother puts him in the river to protect him from the Egyptian ruler. The account in Exodus (2:1–10) describes how the daughter of Pharaoh/Fir`awn comes to the water to bathe and then discovers the crying child in the basket. Assuming that he is one of the Hebrews' children, she takes pity on him. She then has a conversation with the sister of Moses/Mūsā, who arranges for the child's mother to nurse the baby. Pharaoh's/Fir`awn's daughter is unaware of the biological relationship that exists between the woman and the infant, and she pays the mother for her services. After the child grows up, his mother returns Moses/Mūsā to Pharaoh's/Fir`awn's daughter, who names him and takes him as her own son.

In the Qur'an's version of the story, Pharaoh's/Fir`awn's daughter is not mentioned at all, and it is his unnamed wife who helps in Moses's/Mūsā's survival (28:1–14). Unlike the daughter in Exodus, his wife has no direct interaction with the baby's family and she does not name the child. Her one line of dialogue is directed at her husband when she says, "He will be a joy for me and for you. Do not kill him. Perhaps he will be of some use to us, or we may take him as a son" (v.8). The last sentence she speaks in this verse is found verbatim in the Qur'an's story of Joseph/Yūsuf, when his Egyptian master says the same thing to his wife about Joseph/Yūsuf (12:21). Like the Bible, the Qur'an reports that Moses/Mūsā is reunited with his mother through his sister's intervention, but the text does not explicitly state that he is subsequently returned to Pharaoh's/Fir`awn's household. If we are to assume that is what happened, there is an interesting difference in the way the relationship between Pharaoh/Fir`awn and Moses/Mūsā is presented in the two traditions since in the Bible it is more like that of a grandfather and a grandson, while in the Qur'an it would be closer to that of a father and a son.

Questions/Issues

(1) How do the roles of Pharaoh's/Fir`awn's daughter and wife affect the way the story of Moses's/Mūsā's birth is told in the Qur'an and the Bible?
(2) Why might it be that a different member of Pharaoh's/Fir`awn's plays this pivotal role in the two texts?
(3) How can the presence of the exact same sentence in the Qur'an's accounts of the lives of Moses/Mūsā and Joseph/Yūsuf be explained?

42

Prophets

Qur'an 7:65–72; 26:141–59; 11:84–95; 6:83–89; 33:45–48; 33:40; 2:136; 3:84; 4:152; 17:55; 2:253; 33:7–8; 4:69; 20:4; 26:192; 32:2; 16:2; 2:97; 48:27; 28:36; 5:32; 7:101; 9:70; 40:34; 2:91; 25:31; 6:112; 35:25; 3:184; 22:42

The Arabic word for a prophet is *nabī* (plurals, *anbiyā'* and *nabiyyūn*), which appears approximately seventy-five times in the Qur'an and is probably borrowed from Hebrew or another language. It is believed that it has its origin elsewhere because the Arabic root from which the term would be derived has the primary meanings "to be distant, offensive, contradictory," which have no obvious semantic connection with the prophetic office. The Hebrew word for a prophet comes from a root that can describe one who speaks or has been called, and is therefore a better semantic fit. The related Arabic term for prophecy, found five times in the text of the Qur'an, is *nubūwah*.

Almost all of the more than two dozen individuals referred to as prophets in the Qur'an are mentioned in the Bible, but the biblical text does not identify all of them as prophets. Those who are not biblical figures include Hūd (7:65–72), Ṣāliḥ (26:141–159), and Shu`ayb (11:84–95), who are all generally held to be Arabian prophets that predated the time of Islam. The longest list of prophets in the Qur'an is found in the following verses, where eighteen individuals are so designated.

> We gave to him (Abraham) Isaac and Jacob. We guided them both, as we guided Noah before them. Among his descendants were David, Solomon, Job, Joseph, Moses, and Aaron—thus We reward those who do good—and Zachariah, John, Jesus, and Elijah, each of them was among the righteous. Also, Ishmael, Elisha, Jonah, and Lot—each of whom We favored over the worlds—and some of their fathers, descendants, and brothers. We chose them, and We guided them on a straight path. That is the guidance of God, Who leads by means of it whichever

> of His servants He wishes. If they had been among those who associate, what they did would not have succeeded. They are the ones to whom We gave the book, the judgment, and the prophetic office. (6:83–89)

Another biblical figure, not on this list, who is considered to be a prophet in Islam is Adam/Ādam. All of the individuals identified as prophets in the Qur'an are males, and with rare exceptions Muslim commentators on the text have held the view that it teaches that women cannot be prophets.

A succinct description of the role of a prophet is given in a passage that is directed to Muhammad.

> Oh, prophet! We have truly sent you as a witness, a bearer of good news, a warner, one who calls upon God with His permission, and a bright lamp. So bring good news to the believers that they may have great reward from God. Do not obey unbelievers and hypocrites, but ignore their insults and put your trust in God, Who is sufficient as a guardian. (33:45–48)

According to this job description, a prophet is primarily an intermediary between God and people, who is tasked with the responsibility of communicating a divine message. The passage indicates that doing so properly requires a number of qualities and skills, and a prophet will succeed only if he:

(1) is a witness who points beyond himself so that the people will know that the message is God's and not his own,
(2) is a herald of good news who encourages the people to embrace the message,
(3) issues a word of warning that alerts the people about the consequences that await them if they disregard the message,
(4) continues to rely upon God by calling on the deity for assistance,
(5) shines like a light that shows people the proper way to live,
(6) maintains confidence and optimism in the face of rejection and persecution.

The Qur'an's accounts of their lives explain how all of the prophets possessed these traits and remained faithful to the task that God had called them to do, even when they did not succeed. There is a consistent pattern in many of these passages that is sometimes called "the prophetic paradigm" in which the prophet delivers God's message to his people, but they refuse to believe it and are punished for their sin. Sometimes the prophet presents the message in the form of a book, like the Torah given to Moses/Mūsā and the Gospel revealed to Jesus/`Īsā, but usually the prophets verbally remind people to follow the message of submission (*islām* in Arabic) to God's will that had been brought by all the prophets throughout history. The people invariably ignore or distort the prophet's words as the pattern of message followed by rejection continues until the coming of Muhammad, whose followers accepted the text he brought to them. At that point, prophecy came to an end because the message that God had intended for humanity all along was now perfectly preserved in the Qur'an. Because he is the last of their line, Muhammad has been given the title "the seal of the prophets" (33:40).

Despite the special role Muhammad plays as the final prophet, the Qur'an makes it clear that all of the prophets are equally important and no one of them is above the others. In one verse, Muhammad is commanded to tell his followers, "We believe in God, and what has been sent down to us, and what was sent down to Abraham, Ishmael, Isaac, Jacob, and the tribes, and what was given to Moses and Jesus, and what was given to the prophets from their Lord. We make no distinction among any of them, and to Him we submit" (2:136; cf. 3:84; 4:152). At the same time, there are texts that suggest that God has preferred some prophets over the rest. "Your Lord knows what is in the heavens and what is upon the earth. Truly, We have favored some of the prophets over the others, and We gave the Psalms to David" (17:55; cf. 2:253). The reference to David and the Psalms at the end of the verse suggests that one way in which God differentiated among the prophets was by giving a revealed text to some of them and not to others.

The Qur'an also singles out prophets with whom God made a covenant. "Remember when We made a covenant with the prophets—with you (Muhammad), Noah, Abraham, Moses, and Jesus the son of Mary—We made a solid covenant with each of them so that truthful ones might be questioned about their truthfulness. He has prepared a painful punishment for those who do not believe" (33:7–8). Regardless of any differences among the prophets that such passages point to, they should all be held in the same high regard by every believer because they are the first of those who have been blessed by God. "Anyone who obeys God and the messenger will be with those whom God has blessed—the prophets, the truthful ones, the witnesses, and the righteous ones. They are excellent companions!" (4:69).

The most common Arabic root that the Qur'an uses to describe how divine revelation has been transmitted to the prophets is *nazala*, which means "to bring down." The Qur'an itself is sometimes described as a *tanzīl*, or something sent down. "We did not send down (*nazala*) the Qur'an to you so that you might be troubled, but as a reminder to the one who fears God, as a sending down (*tanzīl*) from the One who created the earth and the heavens on high" (20:4; cf. 26:192; 32:2). Islam has traditionally taught that angels were the agents God used to communicate the divine revelation to the prophets (16:2), and Gabriel/Jibrīl is identified as the angelic being through whom the Qur'an was given to Muhammad (2:97). In addition, there is some support in the text for the idea that prophets sometimes receive revelation through dreams or visions (48:27).

As noted above, the people to whom they were sent were often reluctant to believe the messages that the prophets brought them. Because of this hesitancy, a prophet sometimes also produced signs and proofs in order to persuade his audience of the legitimacy of his mission. These signs (*bayyināt* in Arabic) were sometimes miraculous in nature, but even then they did not have the desired effect because the people still refused to believe. The experience of Moses/Mūsā is typical in this regard. "When Moses brought Our clear signs to them, they said, 'This is merely some magic trick. We did not hear any of this from our ancestors of long ago'" (28:36; cf. 5:32; 7:101; 9:70; 40:34). Such was the fate of all of the prophets, some of whom were put to death by those to whom they were sent (2:91). "In this manner, We have given every prophet an enemy from among the sinners. Nonetheless, your Lord is the only guide and helper you need" (25:31; cf. 6:112).

The frequent theme of the rejection of the prior prophets plays an important rhetorical role in the Qur'an because it helps to establish Muhammad as a legitimate holder of the prophetic office. His people's unwillingness to accept him may have been hard for him to bear, but it ironically gave him a status that they did not think he deserved. According to the Qur'an, one of the true marks of a prophet is being rejected by those to whom one is sent, and so his people's inability to believe him placed Muhammad among the ranks of his prophetic predecessors. "If they deny you (Muhammad), know that those before them also denied the ones sent to them who brought them clear signs, scriptures, and a book that enlightens" (35:25; cf. 3:184; 22:42).

The Islamic tradition debated the Qur'anic concept of prophecy and how its legacy would play out within the community. The Shi'is believed that the prophetic prophecy continued after Muhammad's death through the Imams. While the various Shi'i sects differed on the exact nature of the Imam, they agreed that the Imam represented a post-prophetic authority that derived from the household of the prophet (*ahl-bayt*). The Imams were not prophets, in that they were not given new revelation or brought another scripture. However, Shi'i sects did believe that the Imam was divinely guided and many maintained that he was protected from error (*'iṣmah*). The Imams thus played the important function of guiding the community and providing it with religious and, at times, political leadership.

In contrast, the Sunnis held that the post-prophetic legacy and divine protection (*'iṣmah*) were relegated to the larger Muslim community. Prophetic traditions spoke to the idea that the Muslim community would not agree on an error and that the hand of God was over the group. Nonetheless, the Sunnis themselves debated over the nature of divine protection and how it manifested itself within the Muslim community. For instance, the scholastic theologians known as Ash'aris held that the prophets were essentially sinless and divinely protected from mistakes, since they had to properly convey God's message. If prophets sinned, they reasoned, then people would doubt their moral integrity and not follow their call. While post-prophetic figures could not be divinely protected (*'iṣmah*), they could reach the elevated status of saints. However, the traditionalists (*ahl-ḥadīth*) maintained that prophets could commit minor sins but God would protect them from continuing in their error. Post-prophetic figures could become scholars and political leaders, but they should not be seen as sacred and raised to the level of the prophets.

This debate between the scholastic theologians and the traditionalists played out in their interpretation of the various prophet stories, namely, those where the prophets appeared to have sinned or made a mistake. For instance, in the story of Jonah/Yūnus the scholastic theologians understood the prophet's transgression of leaving his people prematurely not as a sin, but rather as an example of leaving what is preferable (*tark al-afḍal*). It would have been better for Jonah/Yūnus to remain with his people and continue to call them to God, but it was not necessarily a sin that he left. Others' opinions contend that Jonah/Yūnus left his people before he officially became a prophet, thus making his mistake a pre-prophetic one. In contrast, the traditionalists asserted that Jonah/Yunus did in fact make a mistake and sinned, but he ended up praying to God and was forgiven. According to this interpretation, Jonah/Yunus was a prophet of repentance, and a model for all believers of how to acknowledge one's shortcomings and seek spiritual renewal. Thus, the story of Jonah/Yūnus, as well as other prophet stories, became a point of contention in how the prophetic legacy would continue within the larger Muslim community.

Questions/Issues

(4) What are some of the similarities and differences in how prophets are viewed in Islam and in Judaism and Christianity?
(5) What is your reaction to the fact that most of the prophets mentioned in the Islamic sources are also biblical figures?
(6) What do you think of the belief that Muhammad is the final prophet?

Further Reading

Ahmed, Shahab. "Ibn Taymiyya and the Satanic Verses," *Studia Islamica*, 87 (1998), 67–124.

Haider, Najam. *Shi'i Islam: An Introduction*, (New York: Cambridge University Press, 2014).

Mirza, Younus Y. "Was Ibn Kathīr the Spokesperson for Ibn Taymiyya?" Jonah as a Prophet of Obedience," *Journal of Qur'anic Studies* 16/1 (2014), 1–19.

Mirza, Younus Y. "Ibn Taymiyya as Exegete: Moses' Father-in-Law and the Messengers in *Sūrat Yā Sīn*," *Journal of Qur'anic Studies* 19/1 (2017), 39–71.

Noegel, Scott B. and Wheeler, Brannon M. *The A to Z of Prophets in Islam and Judaism* (Plymouth, UK: Scarecrow Press, 2002).

43

Queen of Sheba

Qur'an 27:20–44

The Qur'an's account of the visit of the Queen of Sheba to Solomon/Sulaymān in 27:20–44 differs in significant ways from the description of it in the Bible (1 Kgs 10:1–13). As in the biblical narrative, she remains unnamed and the text does not identify the location of her land. Other sources place it in the southern part of the Arabian Peninsula in an area that was strategically located for caravan traffic and was associated with the trade of rare spices

The hoopoe (Arabic, *hudhud*), a member of Solomon's/Sulaymān's retinue of birds, informs him that it has visited the queen and has discovered that she and her people do not worship God because they have been deceived by Satan/Shayṭān. Solomon/Sulaymān then sends the bird back to Sheba to deliver a letter he has written to the queen that orders her and her people to come to him "in submission" (v.31). This command is ambiguous because it could mean either that they should obey Solomon/Sulaymān, or that they should submit to worship of the one God. The message from Solomon/Sulaymān is notable because it begins with the only citation in the text of the Qur'an of the *basmalah*, the superscription that opens every chapter but the ninth one and states, "In the name of God, the merciful and the compassionate." The queen responds by sending Solomon/Sulaymān a gift that he rejects because it is nothing more than an effort on her part to flaunt her wealth.

He then threatens to invade Sheba, but the queen instead pays him a visit during which she is tested twice. The first test entails her throne, which one of the jinn under his command miraculously brings to Solomon/Sulaymān. At the king's command it is disguised, and when she is asked if it is her throne she responds that it seems to be hers. She is then told to enter the palace, and when she does so she thinks it is a pool of water so she bares her ankles. Solomon/Sulaymān then informs her that the palace has a crystal floor, which causes the queen to admit her mistake and surrender herself to Solomon's/Sulaymān's God. The story concludes with her saying, "My Lord, I have truly wronged myself, and I submit with Solomon to God, the Lord of the worlds!" (v.44b). The queen does not explicitly identify the nature of her offense(s).

When compared to the biblical account, the one in the Qur'an appears to have a different purpose. The account of the queen's visit in 1 Kings has a primarily apologetic function as an illustration of the God-given wisdom that Solomon/Sulaymān possesses. This is not the principal aim of the Qur'an's telling of the tradition, which focuses as much, if not more, on the queen as it does on Solomon/Sulaymān.

"The Stories of the Prophets" identify the queen's name as Bilqis, and include some details that further highlight her religious conversion. When her representatives come to Solomon/Sulaymān bearing gifts he rejects them as things he does not need, and he then goes on to say that his only desire is to spread the message of the oneness of God (Arabic, *tawḥīd*). Similarly, once the queen expresses her faith in the God of Solomon/Sulaymān at the end of the story, "The Stories of the Prophets" state that the sun she had worshipped eclipsed within her and her heart was lit by the never fading light of Islam (Ibn Kathīr).

Questions/Issues

(1) What seems to be the main point of the Qur'an's story of the queen's visit to Solomon/Sulaymān?
(2) Identify the main differences between the Bible's and Qur'an's accounts of the visit and explain how they transform the meaning of the story.
(3) What might the queen mean when she states in the Qur'an that she has wronged herself?

Further Reading

Elias, Jamal J. "Power, Prophecy, and Propriety: The Encounter of Solomon and the Queen of Sheba," *Journal of Qur'anic Studies* 11/1 (2009), 57–74.

44

Satan/Shayṭān

Qur'an 2:34–36; 7:11–20; 20:115–20; 12:5; 7:22; 43:62; 4:38; 3:175; 4:60; 17:53; 12:42; 6:68; 18:63; 1:6; 3:51; 15:41; 19:36; 67:22; 24:21; 2:168, 208; 6:142; 7:20–21; 14:22; 59:16; 31:21; 2:268; 20:10; 114:1–6; 35:5–6; 4:120; 17:64; 31:33; 57:14; 5:90–91; 6:112; 2:101–3; 21:82; 38:34–38; 6:71; 23:97; 7:27; 26:210–11, 221–22

Satan/Shayṭān is mentioned approximately seventy times in the Qur'an, and in eighteen other places the plural form "satans" (Arabic, *shayāṭīn*) is found. The only passages that identify Satan/Shayṭān with a particular individual are several accounts of the garden story involving Adam/Ādam and Eve/Ḥawwā', in which Iblīs' character shifts to that of Satan/Shayṭān as he deceives the first couple into eating the fruit of the tree that God has prohibited from them (2:34–36; 7:11–20; 20:115–20). Iblīs' transformation to Satan/Shayṭān in these texts might be a way of calling attention to his disobedience when he rejected God's order to bow down to Adam/Ādam due to his own pride. Prior to this he was known as Iblīs, but after refusing to submit to the divine will he became known as Satan/Shayṭān. This interpretation is in line with Satan's/Shayṭān's role throughout the Qur'an, where he is often portrayed as a figure who tempts human beings rather than as one who is proud.

As the quintessential adversary of humanity, Satan/Shayṭān is consistently presented in unflattering terms throughout the text of the Qur'an. Jacob's/Ya`qūb's warning to his son Joseph/Yūsuf succinctly sums up the antagonistic nature of the relationship between the two sides. "Satan is truly a clear enemy to humankind" (12:5b). God says a similar thing to Adam/Ādam and Eve/Ḥawwā' after they partake of the forbidden fruit in the garden (7:22; cf. 43:62). Anyone who takes Satan/Shayṭān for a friend is an unbeliever who has rejected God (4:38). People are cautioned about several qualities that Satan/Shayṭān possesses that are mentioned in the Qur'an. He frightens the ones who seek his companionship (3:175), and those who are not scared off will be led astray by him (4:60). Satan/Shayṭān causes strife and discord among people (17:53), but perhaps the biggest threat he poses to human beings is that he causes them to forget. The need to remember God and the divine message sent through the prophets is a common theme throughout the Qur'an, and Satan/Shayṭān is viewed as a major cause of why people sometimes forget the deity and neglect to do what they are supposed to do. This is dramatically illustrated in the story of Joseph/Yūsuf when the prisoner he helps to set free does not return the favor by mentioning Joseph/Yūsuf to the king, and Satan/Shayṭān is identified as the one responsible for his lapse. "He (Joseph) said to the one that he thought would be freed, 'Remember me to your lord.' But Satan caused him to forget to mention it to his lord, so Joseph remained in prison for several more years" (12:42; cf. 6:68; 18:63).

God has prepared a way for people to walk upon as they journey through life that is commonly called "the straight path," a phrase that appears nearly three dozen times in the Qur'an (1:6; 3:51; 15:41; 19:36; 67:22). The text warns in places that Satan/Shayṭān also has a way that he tries to entice people to walk down, but it urges them to avoid doing so. "Oh, believers! Do not follow Satan's footsteps. Indeed, Satan commands those who follow his footsteps to do what is immoral and evil. If it were not for God's favor and mercy on you, none of you would be pure. God purifies whomever he wishes. God is the one who hears, and the one who knows" (24:21; cf. 2:168, 208; 6:142). These are the only verses that use the word "footsteps" in the entire Qur'an, and they set up a clear distinction between the way of God and the way of Satan/Shayṭān. They are the two options people must choose from, and they need to be ever vigilant to make sure they opt for the straight path that leads to reward rather than the crooked one whose endpoint is punishment.

The Qur'an teaches that Satan/Shayṭān has various ways of communicating with people in his efforts to persuade them to follow him. Sometimes he speaks directly to them, as he did to Adam/Ādam and Eve/Ḥawwā' in the garden when he convinced them to eat from the forbidden tree (7:20–21; cf. 14:22; 59:16). Elsewhere he calls to them and invites them to enter hell (31:21), or he makes them empty promises. "Satan promises you poverty and he commands you to act immorally, but God promises you mercy and favor from Him. God is all-encompassing and all-knowing" (2:268). An interesting verb that the Qur'an uses to describe how Satan/Shayṭān communicates with humanity is "to whisper," which is found in two of the accounts of the garden story that describe him trying to persuade the first couple to go against the divine order not to eat the fruit (7:20; 20:120). It is also found twice in the final chapter of the Qur'an, which does not refer explicitly to Satan/Shayṭān but there is little doubt that he is the one doing the whispering. "Say (Muhammad), 'I seek refuge with the Lord of humanity, the King of humanity, the God of humanity, from the evil of the one who whispers, the one who slinks, the one who whispers in people's hearts, of the jinn and of humanity" (114:1–6). The Arabic verb "to whisper" is *waswasa*, which is a good example of onomatopoeia because it echoes the sound a person makes when whispering to another. In this way, its use in these passages highlights the sneaky and devious manner in which Satan/Shayṭān attempts to seduce people to follow his way rather than that of God.

An epithet that the Qur'an uses to refer to Satan/Shayṭān is "the Deceiver" (Arabic, *al-gharūr*), which highlights the duplicitous ways by which he tries to tempt people to leave the straight path and become his followers. "Oh humanity! The promise of God is indeed true. Do not let the life of this world deceive you, and do not let the Deceiver deceive you about God. Satan is truly an enemy to you, so take him as your enemy. He calls upon his followers only so that they might be among the inhabitants of the fire" (35:5–6; cf. 4:120; 17:64; 31:33; 57:14). Among the means by which Satan/Shayṭān deceives people are wine, gambling, idolatry, and divination, which the Qur'an identifies as tools he uses to lure the unsuspecting.

> Oh believers! Wine, games of chance, stone idols, and divining arrows are all detestable things from among Satan's works. Avoid them so that you might be successful. Satan only wants to create enmity and hatred among you through wine and games of chance, and thereby prevent you from remembering God and praying. So will you not refrain (from doing these things)? (5:90–91)

As noted above, the plural "satans" appears nearly twenty times in the Qur'an. It is sometimes used to refer to human beings or jinn who act like Satan/Shayṭān by rejecting God and the messengers sent by God. "In this way, We have made an enemy for every prophet—satans from among humanity and the jinn, some of whom inspire others with flowery speech to deceive them. If your Lord had wished, they would not have been able to do it. Leave them and what they invent" (6:112). This verse states that such satanic individuals still submit to divine authority even if they do not realize it because they exist only because God permits it. Elsewhere, the satans are presented as supernatural beings who are skilled in the art of magic that was taught to them by the two Babylonian angels Hārūt and Mārūt (2:102). They are also associated with a biblical character in passages that describe how the satans came under Solomon's/Sulaymān's authority. "And among the satans were those who dived for him and also did other work, and We watched over them" (21:82; cf. 2:101–3; 38:34–38). Throughout the Qur'an, the satans are devious beings who incite people to do evil (6:71; 23:97) and are the companions of unbelievers and those who do evil (7:27). In order to undermine his legitimacy as a prophet, some of Muhammad's contemporaries accused him of having received the Qur'an from satans (26:210–11), a charge he dismissed as patently false (26:221–22).

The book of Job is the only writing that mentions Satan/Shayṭān in the Hebrew Bible, but in that work he has little in common with the way he is presented in the Qur'an. He is a character in the first two chapters of the book, where he convinces God to allow him to inflict pain on Job, but he does not entice Job to sin or disobey the deity as his counterpart in the Qur'an does to humanity at large. In the Bible, he is presented as a member of the divine court, who is charged with the task of monitoring what is happening on earth. In the book of Job he is identified as "the Satan," and so the word functions as a title more than a name. By the time of the New Testament writings Satan has become the personification of evil, a figure who is also referred to by Jesus and others as "the Devil." The Gospels and other Christian texts describe him in ways that put him more in line with the how Satan/Shayṭān is viewed in the Qur'an.

Questions/Issues

(1) What are the most significant similarities between the Islamic view of Satan/Shayṭān and how he is perceived in Judaism and Christianity?
(2) What are the most profound differences among them?
(3) What is your reaction to the presence of the plural form "satans" in the Qur'an?

Further Reading

Awn, Peter. *Satan's Tragedy and Redemption: Iblīs in Sufi Psychology* (Leiden: E. J. Brill, 1983).

Ormsby, Eric L. "The Three Faces of Satan in Islam," in *Deliver Us from Evil*, ed. M. David Eckel and Bradley L. Herling (New York: Continuum, 2008), pp. 28–43.

45

Saul/Ṭālūt

Qur'an 2:246–51

Saul's name in the Qur'an is Ṭālūt, which means "the tall one," and he is mentioned in only one passage in the text. The story involving him is set after the time of Moses/Mūsā, and it opens with the Israelites requesting an unnamed prophet to appoint a king for them so that they might fight in God's way. The prophet is identified as Samuel/Shamwīl in other Islamic sources, where he plays a role similar to that described in the Bible in 1 Samuel 8. When the prophet informs them that God has appointed Saul/Ṭālūt to be their king, the Israelites express displeasure at this choice because he is a person who lacks wealth. The biblical text also calls attention to Saul's/Ṭālūt's humble origin and the Israelite's rejection of him as their leader (1 Sam. 9:21; 10:27).

The prophet responds to their objection by saying that the ark's coming to them is a sign of the legitimacy of Saul's/Ṭālūt's reign as king. This is likely an allusion to the Ark of the Covenant that is mentioned in some of the biblical texts about Samuel/Shamwīl (1 Sam. 4–7). According to the Qur'an, the ark contained a remnant from Moses/Mūsā and Aaron/Hārūn, as well as something from their Lord identified in Arabic as *sakīnah*. This word has the meaning of tranquility or assurance, but it is unclear whether the term refers to a specific object that was placed in the ark. Similarly, the remnant from Moses/Mūsā and Aaron/Hārūn that was in the ark remains unidentified in the Qur'an.

A scene follows in which Saul's/Ṭālūt's army is reduced in size, as a result of a test God administers to them at a river. Saul/Ṭālūt informs them that whoever drinks from the river will not fight with him and those who do not drink will fight with him, except for those who scoop up the water with their hands. This is similar to what happens in a biblical story in Judges 7:4–7, where God reduces the number of troops who will fight with Gideon against the Midianites. Saul/Ṭālūt is left with only a few followers who will fight with him and some of them express concern that they will be unable to defeat their enemies, while others express confidence that in the past small armies have been victorious with God's help. The passage ends with a description of the Israelites' victory over their foes as David/Dāwūd kills Goliath/Jālūt.

The figure of Saul/Ṭālūt is presented in the Qur'an in a way that resonates with certain aspects of Muhammad's prophetic career. As did the Israelites in the case of Saul/Ṭālūt, Muhammad's contemporaries in Mecca expressed doubts about his background and his suitability to serve as a leader. Similarly, Muslim forces sometimes were able to overcome enemies that greatly outnumbered them, as in the Battle of Badr of 624 CE when a Meccan army of more than 1,000 was defeated by Muhammad and 300 of his followers. In this way, the Qur'an's description of Saul/Ṭālūt served to encourage Muhammad and his supporters in times of difficulty and to legitimate him as one who was chosen by God.

Questions/Issues

(1) Identify the most significant similarities and differences in the ways that Saul/Ṭālūt is presented in the Bible and the Qur'an.

(2) What are some ways of explaining the similarities between the Saul/Ṭālūt passage in the Qur'an and biblical story about Gideon in Judges 7?

(3) In both the Qur'an and the Bible, the Israelites are reluctant to accept Saul/Ṭālūt as their king. Why might that be?

Further Reading

Wheeler, Brannon M. *Prophets in the Quran: An Introduction to the Quran and Muslim Exegesis* (London: Continuum, 2002), pp. 254–58.

46

Solomon/Sulaymān

Qur'an 21:78–82; 27:15–44; 34:10–14; 38:30–40; 2:101–3

Solomon/Sulaymān, a king of Israel and a prophet, is mentioned by name seventeen times in the Qur'an. Several sections present various events of his life and reign in some detail (21:78–82; 27:15–44; 34:10–14; 38:30–40). He is described as an "excellent servant" (38:30) and the text calls attention to a number of special gifts and powers that were given to Solomon/Sulaymān, but in some places the passages contain narrative gaps and ambiguities that leave their meanings somewhat unclear.

He and his father David/Dāwūd were granted knowledge by God (27:15) and, in one of the few places where they are mentioned together, their knowledge and wisdom are demonstrated when they resolve a dispute among some people involving sheep that had grazed in a field (21:78–79). A type of knowledge that was granted to Solomon/Sulaymān was the ability to communicate with birds and ants, with one text describing how he smiled and laughed when he overheard an ant telling its fellow ants to run for cover so they would not be inadvertently crushed by Solomon/Sulaymān and his army as they advanced (27:16–19). That text mentions that his forces were comprised of birds, human beings, and jinn (cf. 27:38–42; 34:12–13). Elsewhere, satans are also mentioned as those who came under Solomon's/Sulaymān's authority. "And among the satans were those who dived for him and also did other work, and We watched over them" (21:82; cf. 2:101–3; 38:37). The satans are a category of the jinn who sometimes fail to obey the divine will, and the mention of their diving probably refers to Solomon's/Sulaymān's order that they search under water for precious jewels. When the several references to his power over the wind are included (21:81; 34:12; 38:36), it is clear that the extent of Solomon's/Sulaymān's control in the Qur'an encompasses the sky, the earth, and the sea.

While these traditions about Solomon/Sulaymān do not have biblical parallels, the renown he enjoyed as a builder in the Bible is also a part of his legacy in the Qur'an. "They (the jinn) made for him everything he desired—places of worship, statues, large water basins, and sturdy pots. House of David, be thankful in your work. Few of My servants are thankful" (34:13; cf. 38:37). The biblical account of Solomon's/Sulaymān's reign is found in 1 Kings 1–11, and it ends with an expression of God's displeasure because of the ruler's allegiance to foreign gods (1 Kgs 11:1–13). While Solomon/Sulaymān is not punished personally for his sin, the biblical text presents it as the reason why the unified kingdom that he and his father David/Dāwūd ruled over was divided into two. The Qur'an does not describe Solomon/Sulaymān following other gods, but one passage calls attention to skewed priorities that prevent him from properly worshipping God (38:30–40). The details of the story are not completely clear and commentators differ on its interpretation, but it describes an attraction to horses on Solomon's/Sulaymān's part that causes him to lose perspective. He admits his mistake, asks for forgiveness, and his relationship with God is restored, and it is one of the few texts in the Qur'an to acknowledge that sometimes even prophets must repent of their shortcomings.

Another biblical tradition related to Solomon/Sulaymān that is found in the Qur'an is that of the Queen of Sheba's visit to him (27:20–44). This passage is treated in the entry on her in this book that discusses how it relates to the account in the Bible (1 Kgs 10:1–13). There is a single curious reference to the death of Solomon/Sulaymān in the Qur'an, which recounts how the jinn remained unaware that he had passed away until a small animal or insect gnawed off the bottom portion of the staff he was resting on and his body toppled to the ground (34:14).

"The Stories of the Prophets" sometimes fill in the narrative gaps in the Qur'an by providing details about some of the traditions related to Solomon/Sulaymān. They report that the king was so enthralled with his horses that one day he missed a prayer time. When he realized that his obsession with his horses was preventing him from following God as he wished to, he repented and asked the deity's forgiveness. "The Stories of the Prophets" also explain that the jinn were conscripted to work on Solomon's/Sulaymān's building projects as a punishment for their pride in deceiving people into believing that they were all powerful. Similarly, they explain that the unusual manner in which Solomon/Sulaymān died was a way of teaching the jinn a lesson about God's limitless knowledge, because if they had known the king was dead they would not have kept on working for as long as they did (Ibn Kathīr).

Questions/Issues

(1) In the biblical story of his life, Solomon/Sulaymān is celebrated for his wisdom. Is this also a quality he possesses in the Qur'an?
(2) Why might it be that, unlike in the Bible, the Qur'an does not fault Solomon/Sulaymān for following other gods?
(3) How do its references to his knowing the languages of birds and ants and his having authority over various elements of the created world contribute to the Qur'an's presentation of Solomon/Sulaymān?

Further Reading

Tottoli, Roberto. *Biblical Prophets in the Qur'an and Muslim Literature* (London: Routledge, 2002), pp.35–38.

47

Unbelievers

Qur'an 16:106; 2:108; 4:137; 35:39; 49:7; 4:48, 116; 3:67; 2:135; 10:105; 16:123; 39:3, 38; 2:105; 5:73; 2:256; 10:99–100; 49:13; 5:48

The Qur'an has a number of ways of referring to people who lack what the text maintains is the only true form of faith, or who hold beliefs that are in opposition to those of Islam. In some places it draws upon words that come from the Arabic root *kafara*, which appear approximately 300 times in the text to describe various forms of unbelief. These include blasphemy, disobedience of a divine command, denial or rejection of God, and putting one's faith in idols. The term that is commonly used for this state of unbelief is *kufr*, and the one who engages in it is a *kāfir*. Words from this Arabic root are found in this verse, which describes the dire consequences that await one who rejects true belief. "Those who become unbelievers (*kafara*) after believing in God—except for those who are forced to do so while their hearts remain faithful—and open themselves up to unbelief (*kufr*) will have God's wrath upon them. A great punishment is theirs" (16:106; cf. 2:108; 4:137; 35:39; 49:7).

The other Arabic root that is commonly employed to refer to unbelievers is *sharika*, which carries the meaning "to associate." In theological contexts, it describes the act of associating divinity with something or someone that is not divine and thereby violating the oneness and unity of God. This might be done through idol worship or by ascribing divinity to a human being or a created object. Words from this Arabic root appear more than 100 times in the Qur'an, where the sin of association is referred to as *shirk*, and the one who commits this offense is called a *mushrik*. According to the Qur'an, *shirk* is the only sin that God will not pardon. "God does not forgive associating partners with Him. He forgives anything else as He wishes, but anyone who has associated something with God has committed a grave offense" (4:48; cf. 4:116).

Throughout the Qur'an, a *mushrik* is the opposite of a *ḥanīf*, a radical monotheist who worships only the one God. The latter term appears twelve times in the Qur'an, and in all but one of those passages the word *mushrik* is found in close proximity to it. Abraham/Ibrāhīm is the only person ever identified as a *ḥanīf* in the text, and whenever he is described in this way it is immediately stated that he was not a *mushrik*. "Abraham was neither a Jew nor a Christian. He was an upright person (*ḥanīf*) who submitted, and he was not one of those who associate (*mushrik*)" (3:67; cf. 2:135; 10:105; 16:123). In this verse and elsewhere, the Qur'an contrasts the faith of the true monotheist with the lack of faith of the quintessential sinner.

Most of the passages in the Qur'an that mention unbelievers do not identify them with specific religions or groups, and so it is often difficult to know who exactly is being denounced in a given text. Different groups are undoubtedly being referred to throughout the book, and in general terms it can be said that anyone who rejects God and/or the Qur'an is guilty of *kufr*. Given the religious and social demographics of Arabia during the formative years of Islam, many of these texts would have been originally directed at the polytheists who comprised the majority of the population. Certain passages in the Qur'an suggest that some of those polytheists were actually henotheists, or people who believed in a multiplicity of gods over whom one god ruled supreme. This can be seen in a verse that asks polytheists why they worship more than one god and they reply, "We serve them only in order that they might bring us closer to God" (39:3; cf. 39:38). Whether they were henotheists, polytheists, or idolaters, most of the texts that condemn unbelief are directed against belief systems that were not monotheistic, rather than against Judaism and Christianity.

Nonetheless, there are some passages in the Qur'an that use the Arabic root *kafara* to describe the religions of Jews and Christians. A reference to certain People of the Book who lack faith comes immediately after a verse that speaks directly of Jews. "Those among the People of the Book who do not believe (*kafara*) and those who associate something with God do not like that anything good should be sent down to you from your Lord. But in his mercy God favors whomever He will, and his bounty is endless" (2:105). Similarly, Christians are accused of *kufr* due to their belief in the Trinity. "Those who say that God is the third of three are unbelievers (*kafara*). There is only one God. If they do not desist in what they are saying, the unbelievers (*kafara*) among them will experience a painful punishment" (5:73). Neither of these passages issues a blanket condemnation of Jews or Christians, since they both leave open the possibility that there are believers among them. It is only those "who do not believe" (2:105) and "the unbelievers among them" (5:73) who are singled out, suggesting that those categories do not apply to all Christians and Jews.

It is important to note that the Qur'an never directly accuses Jews or Christians of practicing *shirk*, and therefore being guilty of the only unpardonable offense. This is particularly interesting in the light of Christian beliefs like the Trinity and the incarnation, which holds that Jesus/ʿĪsā was God in human form, which could be viewed as examples of associating something from creation with God. But the Qur'an avoids such a designation for the People of the Book, like Jews and Christians, perhaps because they consider themselves to be monotheists despite any appearances to the contrary.

Unbelief is mentioned frequently in the Qur'an because it posed a significant threat, both externally and internally, to the survival of the early Muslim community. Despite the presence of some monotheists, the population of Arabia at that time was overwhelmingly polytheistic and Muhammad's message of one God threatened to destabilize that status quo. For this reason, he and his followers faced many hardships and much persecution from various quarters. The Qur'an's reminders that unbelievers were on the wrong path and ultimately would be punished for not heeding the message of Islam served to support and encourage Muslims in their efforts to respond to their critics. At the same time, there were potential threats from within. Most of the early Muslims had themselves been polytheists in the not too distant past, and it would have been tempting for them to return to their old ways. Many had been ostracized from their families and communities when they embraced Islam, and turning their backs on Muhammad would have reunited them with their loved ones. The Qur'an's warnings against unbelief would have made them think twice about doing an about-face. As the text cited above states, "Those who become unbelievers (*kafara*) after believing in God ….will have God's wrath upon them" (16:106).

Despite these admonitions against polytheism and similar religious systems, other passages in the Qur'an accept the fact that not all people will embrace Islam and they make it clear that belief should not be forced on a person. A verse that is often cited in this regard is: "There is no compulsion in religion" (2:256). According to this text, faith is a matter of free choice and one is forbidden from imposing a particular form of belief on another person. Another passage says a similar thing, but includes the idea that religious differences are actually a part of God's plan for the world. "Had your Lord so willed, all the people on earth would believe. So can you (Muhammad) force people to become believers? No person can believe, except with God's permission, and

He brings dishonor on those who do not exercise reason" (10:99–100). The last part of that text can be interpreted as a warning against those who might try to go against the divine will by attempting to force someone to follow a particular religion.

Qur'anic teachings like these can be set in the wider context of other passages that recognize and celebrate the diversity that is present in the world. "Oh humanity! We created you male and female and We made you into peoples and tribes so that you might know one another. The most honorable among you before God are the ones who are most pious. Truly, God knows and is aware" (49:13). According to this verse, there is a reason why God created a diverse world—it provides an opportunity for people to know and learn from one another. It issues a challenge to the early Muslim community to transcend the limits of their tribal society and make connections with others beyond their own groups, and in modern times it can be read as an appeal to engage in dialogue with others from different cultures, countries, and religions. A similar point is made in the following verse, which explains that the only competition that should exist among people is in their efforts to outdo one another in goodness. "We have prescribed a law and a way for each of you. If God had willed, He could have made you one community, but He tests you through what He has given you. So race one another in doing good deeds. All of you will return to God, and He will explain to you what you differed about" (5:48b). The passage begins with a reminder that each community has its own law and way of life, and the first half of the verse (not quoted here) makes it clear that this is in reference to Muslims and the People of the Book. People should see their diversity as an opportunity to learn from each other and a reason to act kindly toward one another. Their differences remain, but each group should follow the path it has been given and leave judgment up to God.

Questions/Issues

(1) Are there any similarities between the ways the Qur'an and the Bible view unbelievers?

(2) Which would have been a greater concern for the early Muslim community, the external threat or the internal threat that unbelief posed?

(3) What do you think of the idea that religious differences are part of God's original plan for humanity?

Further Reading

Donner, Fred M. *Muhammad and the Believers: At the Origins of Islam* (Cambridge: Harvard University Press, 2010).

Marshall, David. *God, Muhammad, and the Unbelievers: A Qur'anic Study* (New York: Routledge, 2013).

48

Zechariah/Zakarīyā

Qur'an 6:84–90; 21:89–90; 19:2–15; 3:35–41

Zechariah/Zakarīyā, the father of John/Yaḥyā (identified as John the Baptist in the New Testament), is mentioned by name in four chapters in the Qur'an a total of seven times. He is never explicitly described as a prophet in the text, but that role is implied when he is cited in a passage that lists a number of figures who have been given prophetic status (6:84–90). Another text describes him praying to God for a child and, after God responds by giving him and his wife John/Yaḥyā, it concludes by saying they all acted rightly, called on God in hope and fear, and lived humble lives (21:89–90).

The other two passages that refer to Zechariah/Zakarīyā each link him and his son to the story of the birth of Mary's/Maryam's son Jesus/ʿĪsā. Both texts describe the circumstances surrounding John's/Yaḥyā's conception before explaining how Jesus/ʿĪsā was conceived and born. The first recounts how the elderly Zechariah/Zakarīyā sought God's help in having a son because his wife was unable to bear a child (19:2–15). The deity grants the request and tells him what his son's name will be, but Zechariah/Zakarīyā expresses amazement at this news because of his advanced age and his wife's barrenness. Reminded that it is easy for God to create anything, Zechariah/Zakarīyā then asks for a sign and is told that he will be unable to speak for three days. The actual birth of John/Yaḥyā is not described in the text, and there immediately follows a command from God for him to hold tightly onto the Torah. The passage concludes with God explaining the many gifts he gave to John/Yaḥyā and what a morally upright person he was, and then the story of how Mary/Maryam conceived and gave birth to Jesus/ʿĪsā is related (19:16–33).

The other passage presents a somewhat different version of these events in which Zechariah/Zakarīyā and Mary/Maryam appear together in the same scene (3:35–41). It actually begins with an account of her birth before introducing Zechariah/Zakarīyā into the story. In this narrative, he serves as Mary's/

Maryam's caretaker who is charged with bringing food and other supplies to her in the temple or sanctuary where she resides (the Arabic word for her location is the same one used for the place Zechariah/Zakarīyā is when he prays to God in the scene from chapter 19 discussed above). Each time he comes to her, he discovers that she already has everything she needs. When he asks where the food has come from, Mary/Maryam informs him of its source. "It is from God. Truly, God provides for whomever He wishes without measure" (v.37b). This causes Zechariah/Zakarīyā to immediately utter his prayer for a child, which leads to the same questioning on his part, reassurance from God, request for a sign, and three-day period of muteness that is described in the other passage. While the general outline of the two accounts is the same, and in both of them Zechariah/Zakarīyā ends up with the son he prayed for, the presence and role of Mary/Maryam in the second one transforms the story in an important way. In this case, she provides the motivation for his request because it is her statement that God gives without measure that causes him to appeal to the deity for a child. In this way, the faith of one character becomes the catalyst for the faith of the other.

The only parallel to this material in the New Testament is found in the story of John's/Yaḥyā's conception in the first chapter of the Gospel according to Luke. That account has some elements in common with the traditions in chapters 3 and 19 of the Qur'an, but there are also some intriguing similarities between the passage in the third chapter and a non-canonical Christian text known as the Protoevangelium of James. That work, which comes from the second century CE, also presents Zechariah/Zakarīyā as working in the temple where angels provide Mary/Maryman with a miraculous gift of food.

Questions/Issues

(1) What are the most significant similarities and differences between the Qur'an's two accounts of Zechariah's/Zakarīyā's request for a child?

(2) How does the Qur'an's presentation of Zechariah/Zakarīyā compare with the way his character is described in the first chapter of Luke?

(3) How might the similarities between the Qur'an and the Protoevangelium of James be explained?

Further Reading

Reynolds, Gabriel Said. *The Qur'an and Its Biblical Subtext* (New York: Routledge, 2010), pp. 135–39.

Biblical Citation Index